best
easy
dayhikes
Mount Rainier

Heidi Schneider and Mary Skjelset

FALCON®

Guilford, Connecticut
An imprint of The Globe Pequot Press

A FALCONGUIDE ®

Copyright © 1999 by The Globe Pequot Press
Previously published by Falcon Publishing, Inc.

Falcon and FalconGuide are registered trademarks of The Globe
Pequot Press.

Library of Congress Cataloging-in-Publication Data

Schneider, Heidi, 1978–
  Best easy day hikes, Mount Rainier/ Heidi Schneider& Mary
  Skjelset
          p. cm. — (A Falcon guide)
  Includes index.
  ISBN 1-56044-699-4 (pbk.)
  1. Hiking—Washington (State)—Mount Rainier National Park—
Guidebooks. 2. Mount Rainier National Park (Wash.)—
Guidebooks. I. Skjelset, Mary, 1978– . II. Title. III. Title: Mount
Rainier. IV. Series.

Gv199.42.W22M68617 1999
917.97'7820443—dc21   99-18929
                                                                    CIP

♻ Text pages printed on recycled paper.
Manufactured in Canada
First edition/Third printing

CAUTION
Outdoor recreational activities are by their very nature potentially
hazardous. All participants in such activities must assume the
responsibility for their own actions and safety. The information contained in this guidebook cannot replace sound judgment and good
decision-making skills, which help reduce risk exposure, nor does
the scope of this book allow for disclosure of all the potential haz-
ards and risks involved in such activities.
    Learn as much as possible about the outdoor recreational activ-
ities in which you participate, prepare for the unexpected, and be
cautious. The reward will be a safer and more enjoyable experience.

Contents

USGS Quads iv

Map Legend v

Overview Map vi

What's a "best easy" hike? 1

Ranking the Hikes 2

Leave No Trace 4

For More Information 6

The Hikes

1 Skyline Trail 10

2 Rampart Ridge 15

3 Narada Falls 19

4 Comet Falls 23

5 Trail of the Shadows 26

6 Nisqually Vista 29

7 Alta Vista Summit 32

8 Dead Horse Creek 36

9 High Lakes Trail 40

10 Pinnacle Peak Saddle 43

11 Paradise Glacier 46

12 Snow Lake 50

13 Stevens Creek 54

14 Box Canyon 57

15 Silver Falls 60

16 Grove of the Patriarchs 65

17 Naches Peak 67

18 Dege Peak 70
19 Sourdough Ridge Nature Trail 73
20 Silver Forest 76
21 Emmons Moraine 79
22 Mount Fremont Lookout 82
23 Forest Lake 85
24 Sunrise Rim 89
25 Green Lake 94
26 Tolmie Peak 97
27 Spray Falls 101
About the Authors 104

USGS Quads

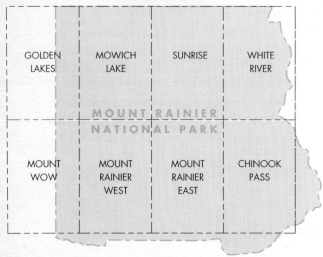

GOLDEN LAKES | MOWICH LAKE | SUNRISE | WHITE RIVER

MOUNT RAINIER NATIONAL PARK

MOUNT WOW | MOUNT RAINIER WEST | MOUNT RAINIER EAST | CHINOOK PASS

Map Legend

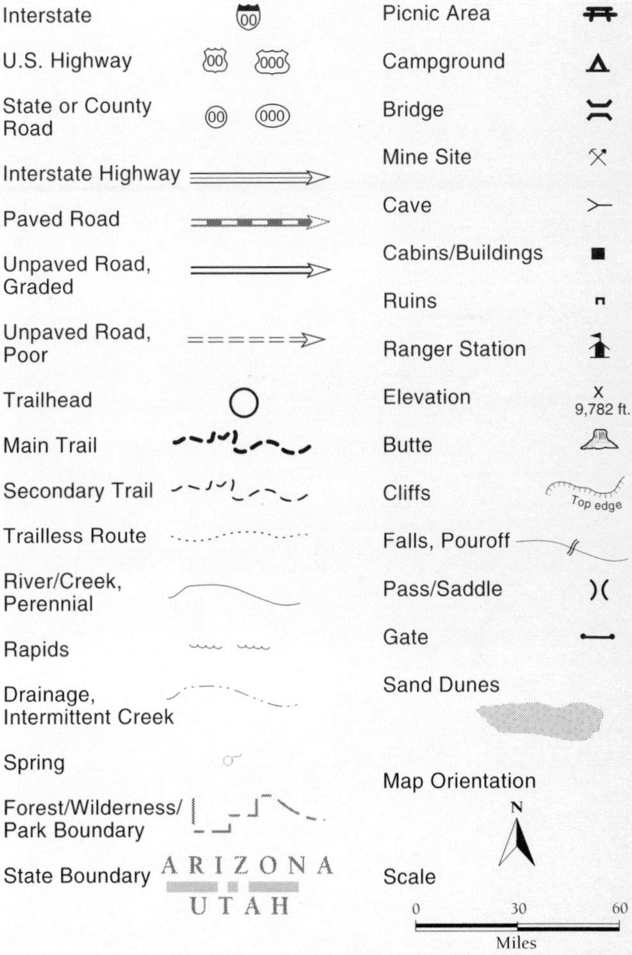

Interstate	🛡00		Picnic Area	🛏
U.S. Highway	(00) (000)		Campground	△
State or County Road	(00) (000)		Bridge	≍
			Mine Site	✕
Interstate Highway	⟹		Cave	⊱
Paved Road	⟹		Cabins/Buildings	■
Unpaved Road, Graded	⟹		Ruins	⌐
Unpaved Road, Poor	=====⟹		Ranger Station	🚩
Trailhead	○		Elevation	X 9,782 ft.
Main Trail	∼∿∼		Butte	🏔
Secondary Trail	∼∿∼		Cliffs	⌒⌒⌒ Top edge
Trailless Route	⋯⋯		Falls, Pouroff	⤳∥
River/Creek, Perennial	⌒		Pass/Saddle	)(
Rapids	∼∼ ∼∼		Gate	•—•
Drainage, Intermittent Creek	⌁⌐		Sand Dunes	▬
Spring	⟜			

Forest/Wilderness/Park Boundary

| ⎮ ⌐ ⌐ ⌐ ⌁ |

State Boundary

A R I Z O N A
▬▬▬▬
U T A H

Map Orientation

N

Scale

0   30   60
▬▬▬▬▬▬▬▬
Miles

v

Overview Map

What's a "best easy" hike?

Best Easy Day Hikes Mount Rainier includes short, less strenuous hikes that we recommend for nice, casual day hikes in the park.

These hikes vary in length but most are short. With a few exceptions, none have seriously big hills. All hikes are on easy-to-follow with no off-trail sections. It is also easy to get to the trailhead of all hikes in this book, and you can get there with any two-wheel-drive vehicle.

Some of the hikes in this book might not seem easy to some hikers but will be easy to others. To help you decide, we have ranked the hikes from easiest to hardest. Please keep in mind that short does not always equal easy. Other factors such as elevation gain and trail conditions have to be considered.

We hope you thoroughly enjoy your "best easy" hiking experiences in Mount Rainier National Park. — *Heidi Schneider and Mary Skjelset*

Ranking the Hikes

The following list ranks the hikes in this book from easiest to hardest.

Easiest   Box Canyon
Trail of Shadows
Silver Forest
Grove of the Patriarchs
Nisqually Vista
Sourdough Ridge Nature Trail
Alta Vista Summit
Dead Horse Creek
Silver Falls
Emmons Moraine
High Lakes Trail
Stevens Creek
Snow Lake
Narada Falls
Spray Falls
Green Lake
Dege Peak
Pinnacle Peak Saddle
Naches Peak
Mount Fremont Lookout
Sunrise Rim
Forest Lake
Paradise Glacier

Tolmie Peak
Comet Falls
Rampart Ridge
Hardest Skyline Trail

Leave No Trace

Going into a national park such as Mount Rainier is like visiting a famous museum. You obviously do not want to leave your mark on an art treasure in the museum. If everybody going through the museum left one little mark, the artwork would be quickly destroyed—and of what value is a big building full of trashed art? The same goes for a pristine wilderness such as Mount Rainier National Park, which is as magnificent as any masterpiece by any artist. If we all left just one little mark on the landscape, the wilderness would soon be despoiled.

A wilderness can accommodate human use as long as everybody behaves. But a few thoughtless or uninformed visitors can ruin it for everybody. All hikers have a responsibility to know and follow the principles of leave no trace. An important source of these principles can be found in the book *Leave No Trace* (available from Falcon Publishing).

The Falcon Principles of Leave No Trace

- *Leave with everything you brought with you.*
- *Leave no sign of your visit.*
- *Leave the landscape as you found it.*

Our wild lands are shrinking, and the number of users is mushrooming. More and more hiking areas show unsightly signs of heavy use. A new code of ethics is growing out of the need to cope with the unending waves of people who want an unspoiled wilderness experience. Canoeists can look behind the canoe and see no trace of their passing. Hikers should strive for the same goal. Enjoy the wilderness but leave no trace of your visit.

Most of us know better than to litter—in or out of the wilderness. Be sure you leave nothing, regardless of how small it is, along the trail or at the campsite. This means you should pack out everything, including orange peels, flip tops, cigarette butts, and gum wrappers. Also, pick up any trash that others have left behind.

Stay on the trail. Avoid cutting switchbacks, and don't walk on plants beside the trail.

Do not pick up "souvenirs," such as rocks, antlers, or wildflowers. The next person wants to see them too, and collecting natural or historical artifacts is against park regulations.

Carry a lightweight trowel to bury human waste 6-8 inches deep and pack out used toilet paper. Keep human waste at least 300 feet from any water source. Better yet, use the restrooms at most trailheads before and after your hike.

Finally, and perhaps most importantly, follow the pack-in/pack-out rule. If you carry something into the backcountry, consume it or carry it out.

Leave no trace—and put your ear to the ground in the wilderness and listen carefully. Thousands of people coming behind you are thanking you for your courtesy and good sense.

For More Information

For a great summary of basic facts on visiting Mount Rainier, call the 24-hour information number (1-360-569-2211) and ask for a free copy of Tahoma News—Visitor Guide to Mount Rainier, a newspaper published by The Northwest Interpretive Association. You also receive a copy of this publication at the entrance station when you enter the park. The paper contains a list of commercial services available in the park, updates on park road construction, campground information, regulations and safety tips, a list of events, and lots more useful information. The Tahoma News will probably answer most of your questions about park services and provide updates on any current situations in the park.

If you have access to the internet, the Mount Rainier website, www.nps.gov/mora, contains a wealth of information. Updated almost daily, this website can probably answer any question you have about Mount Rainier National Park.

Another way to obtain information is to contact one of the visitor centers, ranger stations, or wilderness information centers in Mount Rainier National Park. The list below gives a brief description of how to reach each center from the nearest entrance station and provides a telephone number for each.

Longmire Wilderness Information Center – Phone: 360-569-2211, ext. 3317.
Longmire Museum – Phone: 360-569-2211, ext. 3314.

The center and museum are located in the Longmire Historic District, along Longmire-Paradise Road. From Nisqually Entrance Station on Washington Highway 706 near the southwest corner of the park, drive 6.7 miles to the Longmire complex. The Longmire Wilderness Information Center issues permits primarily for backpacking and has rangers equipped to help you with any questions you might have. The Longmire Museum offers a range of information, such as natural history, cultural history, backpacking, hiking, and trail conditions.

Paradise Ranger Station – Phone: 360-569-2315.

From the Nisqually Entrance Station, drive 15.9 miles east on the Longmire-Paradise Road to the turnoff for Ohanapecosh. Stay to the left and continue up this road to the Paradise complex, 2.2 miles away. This ranger station is open only in the summer.

Jackson Visitor Center – Phone: 360-569-2211, ext. 2328.

From the Nisqually Entrance Station, drive 15.9 miles east on the Longmire-Paradise Road to the turnoff for Ohanapecosh. Stay to the left and continue up this road for 2.1 miles until the Jackson Visitor Center appears on the left. This visitor center operates only during the summer.

White River Wilderness Information Center – Phone: 360-663-2273.

The center is located next to the White River Entrance Station and is open from late May through summer.

Wilkeson Wilderness Information Center – Phone: 360-829-5127.

The town of Wilkeson is on Washington Highway 165 about 35 miles east of Tacoma. The Wilkeson Wilderness Information Center is located in the center of town, in a red caboose next to the library. This center is open from mid-May through the end of summer.

Sunrise Visitor Center – Phone: 360-663-2425.

From the White River Entrance Station, drive 13.8 miles west up the White River Road to the Sunrise complex. The Sunrise Visitor Center, located at the west end of the parking lot, opens in late June and stays open throughout the summer.

Ohanapecosh Visitor Center - Phone: 360-569-2211, ext. 2353.

From Stevens Canyon Entrance Station, drive south 1.8 miles on Washington Highway 123 to the turnoff for Ohanapecosh Campground. The road forks just after you turn in; go right (north) and drive to the Ohanapecosh Visitor Center. This center provides a variety of exhibits and information about Mount Rainier National Park. It opens in the spring and stays open through fall.

Types of Hikes

Loop: Starts and finishes at the same trailhead, with no (or very little) retracing of your steps.

One-way shuttle: A point-to-point trip that requires two vehicles (one left at hike's end and one to get you to the start) or a pre-arranged pick-up at hike's end.

Out-and-back: Hiking to a specific destination, then retracing your steps back to the trailhead.

Skyline Trail

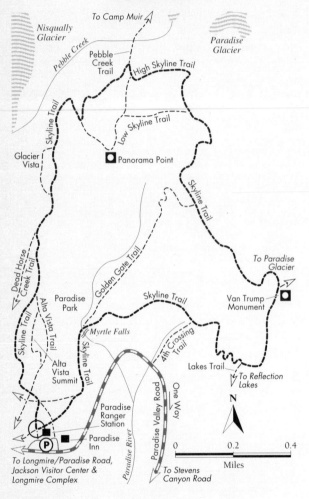

Nisqually Glacier

Paradise Glacier

Pebble Creek

Pebble Creek Trail

High Skyline Trail

To Camp Muir

Skyline Trail

Low Skyline Trail

Glacier Vista

Panorama Point

Skyline Trail

Dead Horse Creek Trail

Golden Gate Trail

To Paradise Glacier

Paradise Park

Skyline Trail

Van Trump Monument

Alta Vista Trail

Myrtle Falls

4th Crossing Trail

Skyline Trail

Alta Vista Summit

Lakes Trail

To Reflection Lakes

Paradise Ranger Station

One Way

Paradise Valley Road

Paradise River

Paradise Inn

N

To Longmire/Paradise Road,
Jackson Visitor Center &
Longmire Complex

To Stevens Canyon Road

0   0.2   0.4

Miles

1
SKYLINE TRAIL

Type of hike: Loop.
Total distance: 5.2 miles (8.7 kilometers).
Best months: Mid-July–September.
Maps: USGS Mount Rainier East; Trails Illustrated: Mount Rainier National Park; Astronaut's Vista: Mount Rainier National Park; Washington, Earthwalk Press Hiking Map & Guide.
Starting point: Skyline Trailhead.

General description: Quite possibly the most popular hike in Mount Rainier National Park, the Skyline Trail is very well maintained, partly paved, and offers a close-up view of the Nisqually Glacier. This is the most strenuous hike in this book.

Finding the trailhead: From the Nisqually Entrance Station, travel 15.9 miles east on the Longmire-Paradise Road. Stay to the left (north) where the road forks, following the road to Paradise. Bypass the visitor center, at 2.1 miles from the fork, and park in the large lot in front of the Paradise Ranger Station at 2.2 miles.

Parking & trailhead facilities: Parking at the Paradise complex can get really hectic. Watch for a flashing sign when you enter the park that indicates whether or not the parking lot at Paradise is full, a common scenario on weekends from 11 A.M. until early evening. You can hope for a vacant spot, but if one does not open up promptly, we suggest finding an alternate hike. If you do find a parking spot, the Paradise complex offers food, phones, restrooms, an inn, a visitor center, and limited supplies.

Key points:

1.1 (1.8) Glacier Vista Trail junction.
1.6 (2.6) Low Skyline Trail junction to Panorama Point.
2.0 (3.2) Pebble Creek Trail junction.
2.8 (4.5) Golden Gate Trail junction.
3.4 (5.4) Paradise Glacier Trail junction and Van Trump Monument.
4.8 (7.7) Myrtle Falls. (Also Golden Gate Trail junction)
5.2 (8.3) Paradise.

The hike: For good reason, more people tour Paradise than any other location on Mount Rainier. The views are absolutely spectacular, the services plentiful, and the trails many. Of all the trails in Paradise, Skyline is the most well known and frequently hiked. As you might guess by the name, the Skyline Trail goes above timberline onto alpine terrain with an awe-inspiring look at the Nisqually Glacier.

For the longest and best view of Mount Rainier, hike this trail clockwise. Start from the Skyline Trailhead in the northwestern corner of the Paradise parking lot. Rather than turning right (east), stay to the left (northwest), heading directly up the mountain. With so many trails, this area is a bit confusing. The signs, however, explicitly point the way.

Stay along the Skyline Trail through all of the intersections. Do not be surprised to see deer. Please, do not feed the wildlife. They have already become very bold from the constant hand-outs.

The trail ascends rather steeply for the next two miles, so prepare for a workout. At 1.1 miles, the Glacier Vista Trail intersects with the main trail. If you would like a slightly closer view of the Nisqually Glacier and a few words on the wonders of glaciation, take this trail to your left (west). It parallels the Skyline Trail for a very short distance and then rejoins it. Continue north for 0.5 mile of switchbacks, at which point you will meet the Low Skyline Trail heading toward Panorama Point. Turn left (northeast) to stay on the Skyline Trail.

Rocky alpine terrain provides the foreground for a close-up view of the mountain for the next 0.4 mile. At the junction to Pebble Creek Trail, 2 miles into the hike, you reach the top of your ascent. This is the path that many mountaineers take on their trek to the summit. If you want to see the Camp Muir snowfield, turn left (north) onto the Pebble Creek Trail. A good glimpse of the path to the top can be had less than 0.5 mile from the turnoff, where Pebble Creek makes a good lunch spot.

Otherwise, stay to the right (east), following the Skyline Trail. You descend steeply along switchbacks in alpine terrain almost all the way to the Golden Gate Trail junction, about 0.8 mile. The Golden Gate Trail provides a shortcut back to Paradise, cutting about 2 miles off the hike length. To stay on the Skyline Trail, bear left.

In 0.7 mile a bizarre bench made of stone serves as a monument to P. B. Van Trump and Hazard Stevens and commemorates their first ascent of Mount Rainier. It also serves as a marker for the trailhead to Paradise Glacier. Sit and relax on the stone slabs before continuing south on the Skyline Trail. Behind the monument, facing south, you have an excellent view of the Tatoosh Range on a sunny day.

The next 1.3 miles of constant descent with sporadic switchbacks leads to Myrtle Falls, an unimpressive but pretty waterfall. Walk to the bottom, a very short side-trip, to see it well. Return to the main trail, which is paved from here on. You should now be able to see Paradise from the trail. A short 0.4 mile takes you back to the trailhead.

Options: If the day is clear, take the Low Skyline Trail to Panorama Point. Less than 0.25 mile of good trail leads to a viewpoint. Here a panoramic picture of the Tatoosh Range and other neighboring mountains is well labeled for your viewing pleasure and insight. A trail from Panorama Point joins the Skyline to the north, so you can easily jump back on the loop.

2
RAMPART RIDGE

Type of hike: Loop.
Total distance: 4.8 miles (7.7 kilometers).
Best months: June–September.
Maps: USGS Mount Rainier West; Trails Illustrated: Mount Rainier National Park; Astronaut's Vista: Mount Rainier National Park; Washington, Earthwalk Press Hiking Map & Guide.
Starting point: Longmire complex.

General description: A short but steep hike up Rampart Ridge for views of Eagle Peak, the Nisqually River, and Mount Rainier.

Finding the trailhead: From Nisqually River Entrance Station, drive 6.7 miles east on the Longmire-Paradise Road to the Longmire complex. Turn right (southeast) into the parking lot. Park here and walk on one of the two crosswalks to the Rampart Ridge Trailhead, across the street from the National Park Inn.

Parking & trailhead facilities: Park in one of the parking lots around Longmire Wilderness Information Center, the Longmire Museum, and the National Park Inn. Parking is a potential problem on sunny weekends and you might have

Rampart Ridge

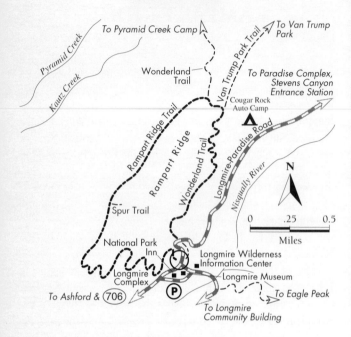

to choose an alternate hike. There are pay phones and restrooms next to the Longmire Museum.

Key points:
0.1 (0.2) Junction with Rampart Ridge Trailhead.
1.8 (2.9) Spur trail to viewpoint.
3.0 (4.8) Junction with Wonderland Trail.
3.2 (5.1) Junction with Van Trump Park Trail.

4.6 (7.4) Longmire-Paradise Road.
4.8 (7.7) Longmire complex.

The hike: This hike is great for those who want a workout, great scenery, and a hike that is snow-free in June. In less than 2 miles, the trail gains 1,280 feet and allows you to peer into the valley you just ventured from and then on into the valley on the other side of Rampart Ridge. The switchbacks are steep, but definitely bearable. Remember to bring plenty of water because this hike has no water sources.

Stay to your left (west) after crossing the street. The first 0.1 mile of the trail is also part of Trail of the Shadows until the Rampart Ridge Trail veers off to the left. The Trail of the Shadows is a self-guided hike around a field of mineral springs.

At the junction with Rampart Ridge Trail, go left (north). For the next 1.7 miles there are relatively steep switchbacks, although they level out at the end just before the viewpoint. This part of the trail is mainly in the trees, but an opening at one point allows a glimpse of Tumtum Peak to the west. After hiking a total of 1.8 miles, you reach a spur trail that goes to a viewpoint. Take a break and enjoy the scenery from the viewpoint. On a clear day, you can to see Eagle Peak, the Nisqually River, the Longmire complex, and the majestic Mount Rainier.

The next 1.2 miles along the ridge are flat and very pleasant. You can see down into the valley on the other side of Rampart Ridge along this section. A glimpse of Kautz Creek can be had 0.2 mile after the viewpoint. You hit the Rampart Ridge Trail junction after traveling 1.2

miles from the viewpoint and 3 miles into your hike. Go right (south) at this junction onto the Wonderland Trail. From then on, the trail loses elevation all the way back to the Longmire complex. About 0.2 mile from the junction with the Wonderland Trail, you'll come to the Van Trump Park Trail splitting off to the left; stay to the right (south) and continue down the Wonderland Trail. At 4.6 miles, cross the Longmire-Paradise Road and continue hiking on the Wonderland Trail all the way to the Longmire complex. There are many signs to point the way on this last stretch.

3
NARADA FALLS

Type of hike: One way, with a vehicle shuttle.
Total distance: 4.5 miles (7.2 kilometers).
Best months: Early July–September.
Maps: USGS Mount Rainier West and Mount Rainier East; Trails Illustrated: Mount Rainier National Park; Astronaut's Vista: Mount Rainier National Park; Washington, Earthwalk Press Hiking Map & Guide.
Starting point: Narada Falls.

General description: A completely downhill hike (with vehicle shuttle) that passes by three waterfalls and runs along the Paradise and Nisqually Rivers.

Finding the trailhead: This hike requires a car shuttle, leaving one car at the end of the hike at the Longmire complex. From Nisqually Entrance Station, drive 6.7 miles east on the Longmire-Paradise Road to the Longmire complex on the right (south). Park one car here and continue on the Longmire-Paradise Road with the other car for 8.4 miles until you see a sign for Narada Falls. Take a right (east) into the parking lot for Narada Falls. The trailhead is on the far east side of the parking lot before the restrooms. Park and walk over the bridge to the Narada Falls Trail on the right (south).

Narada Falls

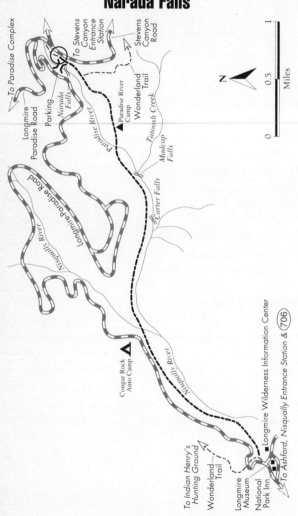

To Paradise Complex

To Stevens Canyon Entrance Station

Stevens Canyon Road

Longmire Paradise Road

Parking

Narada Falls

Paradise River

Paradise River Camp

Wonderland Trail

Tatoosh Creek

Madcap Falls

Longmire-Paradise Road

Carter Falls

Nisqually River

Cougar Rock Auto Camp

Nisqually River

N

0   0.5   1

Miles

To Indian Henry's Hunting Ground

Wonderland Trail

Longmire Museum

National Park Inn

Longmire Wilderness Information Center

To Ashford, Nisqually Entrance Station & 706

Parking & trailhead facilities: There is generous parking and restrooms at the Narada Falls parking lot and the Longmire complex. On sunny weekends, parking is a potential problem and you might have to find an alternate hike.

Key points:

0.2	(0.3)	Wonderland Trail junction.
0.9	(1.4)	Paradise River Camp.
1.5	(2.4)	Madcap Falls.
1.7	(2.7)	Carter Falls.
2.8	(4.5)	Longmire-Paradise Road.
4.5	(7.2)	Longmire complex.

The hike: If you like to hike downhill and love waterfalls, this is the hike for you! You begin at the astonishing Narada Falls, then hike by two other waterfalls, Madcap Falls and Carter Falls. The only disadvantage of this hike is that it requires two vehicles.

From the Narada Falls parking lot, go down the stone steps of the Narada Falls Trail that run along the falls. Narada Falls is wondrous, and on a hot day the cool spray of the falls is very refreshing. Do be careful on the slippery rocks. The first 0.2 mile on the Narada Falls Trail is usually extremely crowded, considering how close the magnificent falls are to the road. Fortunately, the traffic nearly disappears when you join the Wonderland Trail. Go right and head west on the Wonderland Trail. You can hear the Paradise River flowing directly to your right and you will cross it about 1 mile into your hike.

21

Three bridges cross the relatively calm forks of the Paradise River. It is about 0.5 mile from here to Madcap Falls, about 1.5 miles total into your hike. Madcap Falls is where Tatoosh Creek flows into the Paradise River. Instead of dropping straight down, Madcap Falls are at a slight diagonal. The water gushes over the rocks to create a white wonder well worth a photograph.

Soon after Madcap Falls, the gorgeous waters of Carter Falls are marked by a sign. You might come upon a number of people here, considering the close proximity to Cougar Rock Campground.

The next 1.1 miles are a pleasant walk along the Paradise River, despite some metal drain pipes and powerlines along the trail. About 2.8 miles from the beginning of your hike cross another set of bridges, this time spanning the Nisqually River. The waters of the Nisqually River are extraordinarily muddy due to its glacial origin. The waters originate from active glaciers that deposit sediment and grind glacial flour into the river.

After you cross the bridges, climb up to the Longmire-Paradise Road. The Wonderland Trail continues left (west) and is next to a sign indicating that it is 1.6 miles to Longmire, but it is really almost 1.7 miles. In 0.2 mile, you come to another trail junction. Right (north) goes to Cougar Rock Campground, and left (south) goes to the horse ford for the Nisqually River. Continue heading southwest on the Wonderland Trail through old-growth forest all the way to the Longmire complex.

4
COMET FALLS

Type of hike: Out-and-back.
Total distance: 3.8 miles (6.1 kilometers).
Best months: Early July–September.
Maps: USGS Mount Rainier West; Trails Illustrated: Mount Rainier National Park; Astronaut's Vista: Mount Rainier National Park; Washington, Earthwalk Press Hiking Map & Guide.
Starting point: Van Trump Park Trailhead (commonly known as the Comet Falls Trailhead).

General description: A short ascent through enchanting forest to a waterfall that drops over a 300-foot cliff.

Finding the trailhead: From the Nisqually Entrance Station, drive 10.7 miles east on the Longmire-Paradise Road to the Van Trump Park Trailhead and parking lot on the left.

Parking & trailhead facilities: The parking lot at the Van Trump Park Trailhead is often overcrowded on sunny weekends. If you cannot find a space in the parking lot or in the few spaces across the street, you might have to find an alternate hike.

Key points:
0.3 (0.5) Bridge at Christine Falls.
1.9 (3.0) Comet Falls

Comet Falls

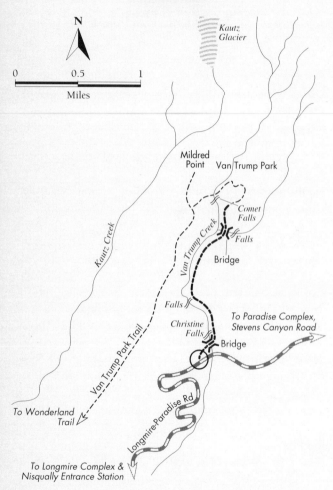

The hike: This hike takes you past two other waterfalls before you reach the highest waterfall accessible by trail in Mount Rainier National Park. In August, salmonberries line the trail for you to enjoy. It is uphill all the way to Comet Falls, but well worth every step.

From the Van Trump Park parking lot, travel up Van Trump Park Trail. Only 0.3 mile into your hike, you come to a bridge over a beautiful falls, the top of Christine Falls. This is also Van Trump Creek. The trail stays mainly in the forest all the way, but it opens up before Comet Falls. At that point, you can relish Van Trump Creek on your left and salmonberries on your right.

You come to a bridge before you reach Comet Falls. The trail seems to fork before the bridge, but stay to the left. The trail to the right (east) is a small spur trail that wraps around the bend to below an unnamed falls. You also have a nice view of the falls from the bridge.

When you reach your first view of Comet Falls, 1.7 miles from the beginning of your hike, several viewing areas await. The white waters of Comet Falls do, in fact, resemble the tail of a comet. The spectacular falls are visible from the bottom of the switchbacks, but you have to travel 0.2 mile up the steep switchbacks adjacent to the falls to get a close-up view of the falls. You might even get a little wet!

5
TRAIL OF THE SHADOWS

Type of hike: Loop.
Total distance: 0.7 mile (1.1 kilometers).
Best months: May–October.
Maps: USGS Mount Rainier East; Trails Illustrated: Mount Rainier National Park; Astronaut's Vista: Mount Rainier National Park; Washington, Earthwalk Press Hiking Map & Guide.
Starting point: Longmire complex.

General description: A 20-minute stroll around the Longmire meadow, with interpretive signs about the Longmire family and their stake in the park.

Finding the trailhead: From the Nisqually Entrance Station, drive 6.7 miles east on the Longmire-Paradise Road to the Longmire Complex on the right (east). Park in one of the many spaces available, then cross the road along one of the two crosswalks to find the trailhead.

Parking & trailhead facilities: Park in one of the parking lots around Longmire Wilderness Information Center, the Longmire Museum, and the National Park Inn. Parking is a potential problem on sunny weekends and you might have to choose an alternate hike. There are pay phones and restrooms next to the Longmire Museum.

Trail of the Shadows

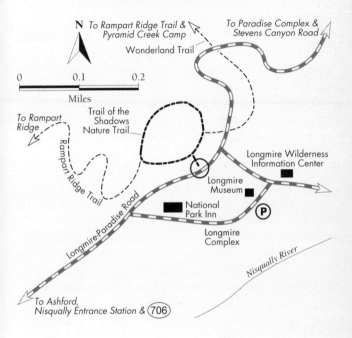

Key points:

0.1 (0.2) Masonry spring.
0.2 (0.3) Longmire's cabin.
0.2 (0.3) Iron Mike.
0.5 (0.8) Travertine Mound.

The hike: History buffs who enjoy casual strolls will thoroughly enjoy this hike. The trail winds around an enchanting meadow, leading to many informative stations. The theme of the stations is James Longmire, his crusade for a natural health spa, and his love of the mountain.

Starting to the right (north), the first stop is a work of stone masonry with bubbling water, said in the nineteenth century to cure any illness. As the sign ironically reads, do NOT drink this water; it can make you very ill.

At the next stop, 0.2 mile into the hike, the cabin that Longmire built still has the original furniture also constructed by Longmire. Next door is IronMike, a spring that is tinted orange by iron minerals.

About 0.5 mile from the trailhead, a short side trip reveals the travertine mound, another orange mass bursting with mineral water. A bench here offers a nice place to sit and view the meadow.

The home stretch of the loop includes a variety of interesting wild vegetation. After completing the loop, cross the road to your car and the large present-day Longmire complex. Notice the great disparity between the present-day edifices and the shadows of the past.

6
NISQUALLY VISTA

Type of hike: Out-and-back.
Total distance: 1.2 miles (1.9 kilometers).
Best months: Early July–September.
Maps: USGS Mount Rainier East; Trails Illustrated: Mount Rainier National Park; Astronaut's Vista: Mount Rainier National Park; Washington, Earthwalk Press Hiking Map & Guide.
Starting point: Dead Horse Creek Trailhead.

General description: A short hike through beautiful forest overlooking the Nisqually Glacier.

Finding the trailhead: From the Nisqually Entrance Station, drive 15.9 miles east on the Longmire-Paradise Road to the turnoff for the Ohanapecosh Area. Stay to the left and continue on the Longmire-Paradise Road for 2.1 miles. Park in the parking lot in front of the Jackson Visitor Center.

Parking & trailhead facilities: Parking at the Paradise complex can get really hectic. Watch for a flashing sign when you enter the park that indicates whether or not the parking lots at Paradise are full. Even if all of the parking lots are full, you can drive another 0.1 mile up the road to the parking lot in front of the Paradise Ranger Station and the Paradise

Nisqually Vista

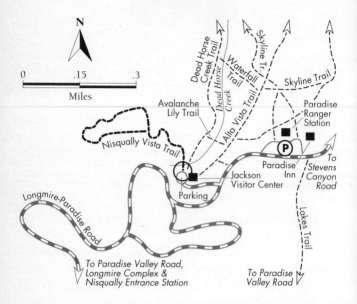

Inn. Bathrooms are located inside the Jackson Visitor Center and in the upper lot next to the Paradise Ranger Station. The Paradise complex offers food, phones, restrooms, an inn, a visitor center, and limited supplies.

Key points:

0.3 (0.5) Beginning of loop.
0.6 (1.0) First viewpoint of Nisqually Glacier.
0.9 (1.4) End of loop.
1.2 (1.9) Dead Horse Creek Trailhead.

The hike: This is a great hike for kids and adults alike. The trail takes you through beautiful forested areas and wonderful meadows to an overlook of the Nisqually Glacier. The Nisqually Vista Trail is a self-guiding trail, but the National Park Service offers a guided tour of this hike. Inquire inside the Jackson Visitor Center for more information. It is downhill all the way to the lookout and then uphill back to the parking lot, but both gradients are gradual.

From wherever you are in the Jackson Visitor Center parking lot, head to the northwest end of the parking lot. Look for a trail sign for the Dead Horse Creek Trail. Go left (northwest) onto the Nisqually Vista Trail. The trail forks less than 0.3 mile down the trail. Go right (southwest). Halfway through the loop and halfway through your hike, you come to a viewpoint. There are three viewpoints total and the last one has a display on the Nisqually Glacier.

From all the viewpoints, you can see where the Nisqually River comes out of the Nisqually Glacier and the massive moraine the glacier has dug out. The Nisqually Glacier is currently advancing at about 6 inches per day. At one point, the glacier extended all the way to Ricksecker Point, which you might have seen on the way from the Longmire complex to the Paradise complex. It is visible from the only bridge between the two areas.

The remainder of the loop is a little over 0.3 mile long, wandering through quaint forest with meadows of lupine and bistort (commonly called bottlebrush). When you come to the end of the loop, stay to the left, toward the visitor center. Enjoy a leisurely hike back to the parking lot.

7
ALTA VISTA SUMMIT

Type of hike: Out-and-back.
Total distance: 1.6 miles (2.6 kilometers).
Best months: Early July–September.
Maps: USGS Mount Rainier East; Trails Illustrated: Mount Rainier National Park; Astronaut's Vista: Mount Rainier National Park; Washington, Earthwalk Press Hiking Map & Guide.
Starting point: Jackson Visitor Center.

General description: A short hike up to the Alta Vista Summit, where you have an excellent view of Paradise Park and the Tatoosh Range.

Finding the trailhead: From the Nisqually Entrance Station, drive 15.9 miles east on the Longmire-Paradise Road to the turnoff for the Ohanapecosh Area. Stay to the left and continue on the Longmire-Paradise Road for 2.1 miles. Park in the parking lot in front of the Jackson Visitor Center.

Parking & trailhead facilities: Parking at the Paradise complex can get really hectic. If you do find a parking spot, the Paradise complex offers food, phones, restrooms, an inn, a visitor center, and limited supplies. Watch for a flashing sign when you enter the park that indicates whether or not the

Alta Vista Summit

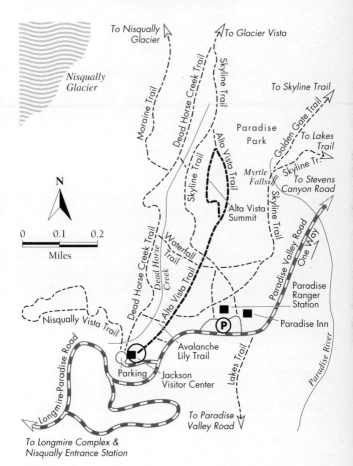

parking at Paradise is full. If all of the parking lots are full, the parking lot in front of the visitor center is also likely to be full. In this case, you can drive another 0.1 mile up the road to the parking lot in front of the Paradise Ranger Station and the Paradise Inn. Restrooms are located inside the Jackson Visitor Center and in the upper lot next to the Paradise Ranger Station.

Key points:

0.1 (0.2) Junction with Avalanche Lily Trail.
0.2 (0.3) Junction with Waterfall Trail.
0.5 (0.8) Beginning of loop.
1.1 (1.8) End of loop.
1.6 (2.6) Jackson Visitor Center.

The hike: This hike is excellent for children. It is short, scenic, and gives you a little taste of Mount Rainier National Park. If you take this hike in July or August, an abundance of wildflowers will line the trails. Please preserve the fragile meadows where the flowers grow by staying on the trail. Expect to see an abundance of people on this popular trail.

The trail, paved and well maintained, begins directly west of the Jackson Visitor Center. No trailhead sign marks the beginning of the Alta Vista Trail, but follow the paved steps that head north for just a few steps and you will come to a display of trails in the Paradise area. Do not take the spur trail heading to the right (east); it leads to the Paradise Ranger Station.

Head north on the Alta Vista Trail for 0.1 mile to the Avalanche Lily Trail, which runs from the Dead Horse Creek

Trail to the Paradise Ranger Station. Continue straight and immediately pass a small spur trail on the left that connects with the Avalanche Lily Trail heading southwest. Stay on the Alta Vista Trail traveling north. There are also detailed signs to help you stay on the Alta Vista Trail.

After another 0.1 mile, the Waterfall Trail goes left (west) to the Dead Horse Creek Trail and right to the Skyline Trail. Again, stay on the Alta Vista Trail heading north. Very soon after this trail junction, you come to the Skyline Trail. Again, stay on the Alta Vista Trail. At this point, the trail grade turns markedly steep. Pace yourself.

About 0.5 mile into your hike, you come to the beginning of the loop to the Alta Vista Summit. Go left (northwest) toward the summit with the help of a sign pointing in the correct direction. The trail climbs to the Alta Vista Summit. Below, Paradise Park is to the right (east). In good weather, tons of people mill about below on other Paradise Trails. Turn around and look to the south for a fabulous view of the Tatoosh Range. The jutting peaks take your breath away.

You can enjoy the view from one of many rock benches here. Please preserve the meadows by staying on the trail or in a designated rest area.

When you have enjoyed yourself to the fullest, complete your loop by continuing north on the Alta Vista Trail or simply turn around and go back the way you came. If you decide to complete the loop, you reach the east side of the loop 0.1 mile from the summit, over 0.8 mile from the Jackson Visitor Center. Turn right and head south on the east side of the Alta Vista Trail until you come to where you began the loop, now 1.1 miles into your hike. From this point, head back the way you came.

8
DEAD HORSE CREEK

Type of hike: Loop hike.
Total distance: 2.3 miles (3.7 kilometers).
Best months: Early July–September.
Maps: USGS Mount Rainier East; Trails Illustrated: Mount Rainier National Park; Astronaut's Vista: Mount Rainier National Park; Washington, Earthwalk Press Hiking Map & Guide.
Starting point: Jackson Visitor Center parking lot.

General description: A short spur trail that connects with the Skyline Trail and has great views of the Tatoosh Range, Mount Rainier, and the Nisqually Glacier.

Finding the trailhead: From the Nisqually Entrance Station, drive 15.9 miles east on the Longmire-Paradise Road to the turnoff for the Ohanapecosh Area. Stay to the left and continue on the Longmire-Paradise Road for 2.1 miles. Park in the parking lot in front of the Jackson Visitor Center.

Parking & trailhead facilities: Parking at the Paradise complex can get really hectic. Watch for a flashing sign when you enter the park that indicates whether or not the parking at Paradise is full. If all of the parking lots are full, you can drive another 0.1 mile up the road to the parking lot in front

Dead Horse Creek

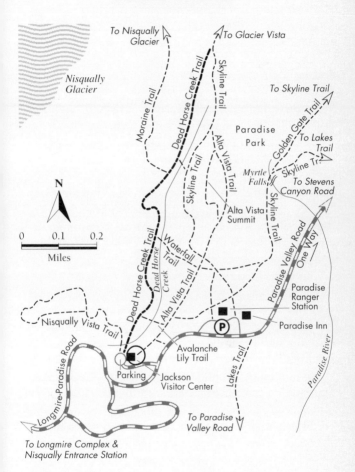

Nisqually
Glacier

To Nisqually
Glacier

To Glacier Vista

To Skyline Trail

Moraine Trail

Dead Horse Creek Trail

Skyline Trail

Alta Vista Trail

Paradise Park

Golden Gate Trail

To Lakes
Trail

Skyline Tr.

Myrtle
Falls

To Stevens
Canyon Road

N

0   0.1   0.2

Miles

Skyline Trail

Alta Vista
Summit

Skyline Trail

Waterfall
Trail

Dead Horse
Creek

Alta Vista Trail

Paradise Valley Road
One Way

Paradise
Ranger
Station

Nisqually Vista Trail

Dead Horse Creek Trail

Avalanche
Lily Trail

Paradise Inn

Paradise River

P

Parking

Jackson
Visitor Center

Lakes Trail

Longmire-Paradise Road

To Paradise
Valley Road

To Longmire Complex &
Nisqually Entrance Station

of the Paradise Ranger Station and the Paradise Inn. Restrooms are located inside the Jackson Visitor Center and in the upper lot next to the Paradise Ranger Station. The Paradise complex offers food, phones, restrooms, an inn, a visitor center, and limited supplies.

Key points:

0.1 (0.2) Junction with Avalanche Lily Trail.
0.4 (0.6) Junction with Waterfall Trail.
0.7 (1.1) Junction with Moraine Trail.
1.1 (1.8) Junction with Skyline Trail.

The hike: If you desire to hike the Skyline Trail, but want a more gradual ascent, you should consider taking this trail. This is also a shorter alternative to the Skyline Trail. In August, the trail is lined with wildflowers, from lupine to Lewis monkeyflower. Please preserve these flowers by staying on designated trails.

Head to the west end of the parking lot and look for a trail sign for the Dead Horse Creek Trail. Stay to the right heading north on the Dead Horse Creek Trail. The trail goes through beautiful, serene forest. Although the Paradise area is extremely busy, this trail receives less use than many other trails, adding to the tranquility of your hike.

Wildlife is commonly seen along the trail. Deer, grouse, and marmots often venture into this area. Remember not to feed these wild animals because they need to remain self-sufficient to survive in their natural habitat. Also, it is illegal to feed the wildlife in Mount Rainier National Park.

Continue going north and ignore the two trails splitting right, the Avalanche Lily Trail (in 0.1 mile) and the Waterfall Trail (almost 0.4 mile into the hike). Both of these trails lead to the Paradise Ranger Station and the Paradise Inn. There are signs at every intersection to help you stay on the Dead Horse Creek Trail. The Nisqually Glacier is visible to the left (west). Please use the rock benches to minimize your impact on the fragile subalpine meadows while enjoying the view.

After 0.7 mile the trail intersects with the Moraine Trail. Stay to the right (northeast). Not far from this junction, look for a small spur trail to the right connecting with the Skyline Trail. Stay on the main trail.

The trail is considerably steeper at this point, but you only have 0.4 mile left to the end of the trail, over 1.1 miles into your hike. The end of Dead Horse Creek Trail is the Skyline Trail. You have the option of hiking down the way you just came or making a loop by following the Skyline Trail. If you choose to take the Skyline Trail, follow the signs to stay on the Skyline Trail until you see a sign for the visitor center. Then follow the signs that point to the visitor center.

9
HIGH LAKES TRAIL

Type of hike: Loop.
Total distance: 2.7 miles (4.3 kilometers).
Best months: Mid-July–September.
Maps: USGS Mount Rainier East; Trails Illustrated: Mount Rainier National Park; Astronaut's Vista: Mount Rainier National Park; Washington, Earthwalk Press Hiking Map & Guide.
Starting point: Reflection Lakes.

General description: A short loop with a great view of the Tatoosh Range and Reflection Lakes.

Finding the trailhead: From Stevens Canyon Entrance Station, drive 18.1 miles west on Stevens Canyon Road to Reflection Lakes.

Parking & trailhead facilities: Park in the parking lot in front of Reflection Lakes. Parking is a potential problem on sunny weekends and you might have to choose an alternate hike. If you need additional services or supplies, the Paradise complex has a snack bar, restrooms, a ranger station, a gift shop, and a post office.

High Lakes Trail

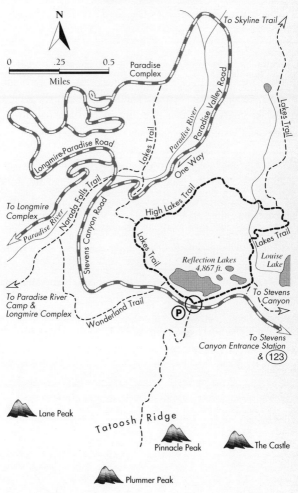

N

0   .25   0.5

Miles

Paradise Complex

Paradise Valley Road

Lakes Trail

Paradise River

One Way

Longmire-Paradise Road

To Longmire Complex

To Skyline Trail

Lakes Trail

Narada Falls Trail

Paradise River

Stevens Canyon Road

High Lakes Trail

Lakes Trail

Reflection Lakes 4,867 ft.

Lakes Trail

Louise Lake

To Paradise River Camp & Longmire Complex

Wonderland Trail

P

To Stevens Canyon

To Stevens Canyon Entrance Station & (123)

Lane Peak

Tatoosh Ridge

Pinnacle Peak

The Castle

Plummer Peak

41

Key points:
0.7 (1.1) High Lakes Trail Junction.
1.9 (3.0) Junction with Lakes Trail.
2.4 (3.8) Wonderland Trail Junction.
2.7 (4.3) Reflection Lakes.

The hike: This easy hike explores the area around Reflection Lakes. The trail takes you part-way up Mazama Ridge, gaining just enough elevation to enjoy an excellent view of the Tatoosh Range.

From the Reflection Lakes parking lot, walk east along Stevens Canyon Road until you hit the Lakes Trail. Go left (northeast) onto the Lakes Trail. Continue on the Lakes Trail up the south side of Mazama Ridge—a relatively steep but short section—to the High Lakes Trail. After traveling 0.7 mile, you reach the High Lakes Trail.

Turn left (west) onto the High Lakes Trail, which is mostly downhill or flat with many opportunities to view the Tatoosh Range. You can see Pinnacle Peak, Plummer Peak, and Unicorn Peak jutting toward the sky.

After traveling 1.2 miles on the High Lakes Trail, you come back to the Lakes Trail. Go left (south) and downhill on the Lower Lakes Trail for 0.5 mile until you meet the Wonderland Trail. Stay to the left and head toward Reflection Lake for the next 0.2 mile to Stevens Canyon Road. Walk 0.1 mile along the road to where you parked.

10
PINNACLE PEAK SADDLE

Type of hike: Out-and-back.
Total distance: 2.6 miles (4.2 kilometers).
Best months: Late July–September.
Maps: USGS Mount Rainier East; Trails Illustrated: Mount Rainier National Park; Astronaut's Vista: Mount Rainier National Park; Washington, Earthwalk Press Hiking Map & Guide.
Starting point: Pinnacle Peak Trailhead, across from Reflections Lake.

General description: A short climb up to the saddle between Pinnacle Peak and Plummer Peak, with great views of Mount Rainier along the trail and at the saddle.

Finding the trailhead: From the Stevens Canyon Entrance Station, drive about 18 miles west on Stevens Canyon Road until you see Reflection Lake on the right. You can park anywhere along Reflection Lake to get to the Pinnacle Peak Trailhead, but it would be a good idea to go as far west as possible. Look for the trailhead on the left (south) side of the road near the end of the lake.

Parking & trailhead facilities: Park in the parking lot in front of Reflection Lakes. Parking is a potential problem on sunny weekends and you might have to choose an alternate hike.

Pinnacle Peak Saddle

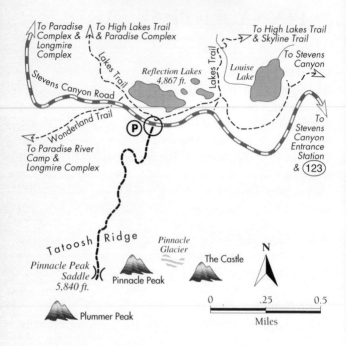

If you need additional services or supplies, the Paradise complex has a snack bar, restrooms, a ranger station, a gift shop, and a post office.

The hike: This hike is uphill the whole way to the saddle. Wildflowers, such as lupine and magenta paintbrush, often grow along the trail in July and August. Many pikas inhabit the rockfields along the trail, squeaking their warnings as people pass by. From the saddle, you have an excellent view of Mount Rainier. Hope for a clear day.

There are no tricky turns or junctions on this trail. Simply start from the trailhead, directly across from the west end of Reflection Lakes, and hike all the way to the saddle. The first half of the trail is in the forest and climbs gradually. Keep in mind that once you hit the first rockfield, the trail becomes steep and rocky. Snow lingers on these rockfields late into the summer, and sturdy hiking boots are required.

Once you reach the saddle, you can see to the south boundary of the park and all the way to the town of Packwood. Plummer Peak resides to your right (west) and Pinnacle Peak rises on your left (east). To the southeast, you can see both Unicorn Peak and the Castle, and to the southwest Wahpenayo Peak is visible. Enjoy the amazing view before heading back the way you came.

11
PARADISE GLACIER

Type of hike: Out-and-back.
Total distance: 6.4 miles (10.2 kilometers).
Best months: Mid July–September.
Maps: USGS Mount Rainier East; Trails Illustrated: Mount Rainier National Park; Astronaut's Vista: Mount Rainier National Park; Washington, Earthwalk Press Hiking Map & Guide.
Starting point: Skyline Trailhead.

General description: A steady climb to a snowfield at the foot of a small glacier.

Finding the trailhead: From the Nisqually Entrance Station, travel 15.9 miles east on the Longmire-Paradise Road to where the road forks. Stay to the left (north) along the road to Paradise. Bypass the visitor center, 2.1 miles from the fork, and park in the large parking lot in front of the Paradise Ranger Station, at 2.2 miles.

Parking & trailhead facilities: Parking at the Paradise complex can get really hectic. Watch for a flashing sign when you enter the park that indicates whether or not the parking lots at Paradise are full—a common scenario on weekends from 11 A.M. until early evening. You can hope for a vacant

Paradise Glacier

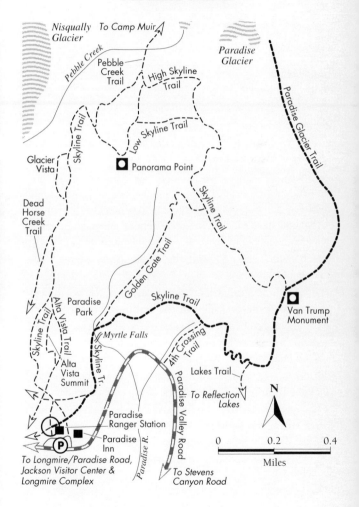

spot, but if one does not open up promptly, consider choosing an alternate hike. If you do find a parking spot, the Paradise complex offers food, phones, restrooms, an inn, a visitor center, and limited supplies.

Key points:
0.4 (0.6) Myrtle Falls and Golden Gate Trail junction.
0.7 (1.1) 4th Crossing Trail junction.
1.4 (2.2) Lakes Trail junction.
1.8 (2.9) Paradise Glacier Trail junction and Van Trump Monument.
3.2 (5.1) Paradise Glacier.

The hike: The ice caves of yesteryear that used to draw many to this trail have melted with the general increase in global temperature. This means a less sensational hike, but it also means fewer passersby and the same spectacular view as before.

Start hiking along the Skyline Trail from the northwestern corner of the parking lot; the trailhead should be well marked. Proceed to the right (east), counterclockwise along the loop. Many trails congest this area, but just follow the Skyline Trail signs eastbound, and you will reach your destination.

After hiking gradually uphill along a wide, paved trail for 0.4 mile, you arrive at Myrtle Falls. The path to the bottom of the falls is short but steep, and offers a closer look at the falls. Back on the main trail, cross Edith Creek, the source of Myrtle Falls, and stay to the right beyond the Golden Gate Trail junction.

Climb steadily, switching-back occasionally, for 0.3 mile, at which point the 4th Crossing Trail joins in. Stay to the left, continuing to head east. Much like previous parts of the trail, this stretch climbs moderately through subalpine forest. You soon reach the Lakes Trail junction, 1.4 miles into the hike. Once again, stay to the left, heading northeast.

The trail turns north, and 0.4 mile from the Lakes Trail junction arrives at a fork marked by a stone bench. This firm resting spot was erected by the Mountaineers and the Mazamas as a tribute to Hazard Stevens and Philamon Beecher Van Trump. The monument marks the campsite from which the two made the first recorded ascent of Mount Rainier. It also marks the Paradise Glacier Trail junction.

Turn right (east) onto the Paradise Glacier Trail. From here, the ascent is gradual, but it leads into alpine terrain. Even in late summer, you will encounter quite a bit of snow, so wear boots if you have them. The trail ends in a snowfield, so hike only as far as you feel comfortable. No sign marks the end of the maintained trail. Cairns guide you to the snowfield where the ice caves once were.

A good view of Paradise Glacier is not the reason to hike this trail. The snowfield, however, is a good place to play name that glacier. Facing north up the trail, you have a close view of the glaciated mountain, to the east are the headwaters of Stevens Creek, and directly behind you (south) is an amazing view of the Tatoosh Range, the Goat Rocks, and Mount Adams.

When you are ready, return to Paradise along the same trail.

12
SNOW LAKE

Type of hike: Out-and-back.
Total distance: 2.5 miles (4 kilometers).
Best months: Mid July–September.
Maps: USGS Mount Rainier East; Trails Illustrated: Mount Rainier National Park; Astronaut's Vista: Mount Rainier National Park; Washington, Earthwalk Press Hiking Map & Guide.
Starting point: Snow Lake Trailhead.

General description: Perfect for children, this two-hour hike passes one lake and ends at another lake cradled in a glacial cirque.

Finding the trailhead: From Stevens Canyon Entrance Station, drive 15.5 miles west along the winding Stevens Canyon Road. A small parking lot on the left (south) marks the trailhead to Snow Lake.

Parking & trailhead facilities: The Snow Lake Trailhead has a small parking lot, not always adequate for the number of hikers. If you need other services, such as restrooms, food, equipment, and lodging, the Paradise complex has all of these.

Snow Lake

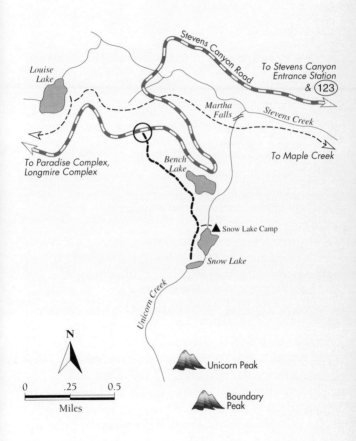

Louise
Lake

Stevens Canyon Road

To Stevens Canyon
Entrance Station
& 123

Martha
Falls

Stevens Creek

To Paradise Complex,
Longmire Complex

To Maple Creek

Bench
Lake

▲ Snow Lake Camp

Snow Lake

Unicorn Creek

N

0   .25   0.5
Miles

Unicorn Peak

Boundary
Peak

Key points:
0.7 (1.1) Bench Lake.
1.2 (1.9) Snow Lake Camp.
1.3 (2.1) Snow Lake.

The hike: Trees obscure the Snow Lake Trailhead. After parking, walk to the eastern corner of the lot to find the trail, heading south. The trail immediately begins to ascend rather steeply, but do not worry, it eventually levels off and even descends as it crosses a few ridges throughout the hike.

The trail wanders 0.75 mile through silver subalpine forest to a junction with the trail for Bench Lake on the left (east). The path down to the lake is steep, but worth the struggle, particularly if you fish. We saw many fish jump in Bench Lake, and, as is true throughout the park, fishing is free and with few limits.

Returning to the main trail, you only have 0.5 mile of hiking to reach Snow Lake. When you arrive at the mountain meadow, turn around. This area offers a beautiful view of Mount Rainier. The last 0.2 mile of trail slopes upward until you see the lovely lake. The peaks of the Tatoosh Range frame the lake, and glacial waters cascade down their flanks into the ice-cold, turquoise waters.

If you would like to camp here or see the marvelous view from the campsites, turn left (east) at the fork in the trail; a sign points the way. Descend for less than 0.2 mile until the trail crosses a stream out of Snow Lake. Hop from log to log to cross the stream, but be careful—some of these logs are not quite as stable as they appear. Directly across the stream is Snow Lake Camp. The toilet is immediately to your left, and the campsites are farther southeast along the lake. Campsite 1 sits on a small peninsula with a view of Unicorn Peak across the lake. A jutting rock makes for a great place to jump in the freezing waters for a refreshing dunk or a painful swim.

You can also follow the path to the right (southwest) at the fork before the lake. This path runs 0.3 mile to a small lake access point. If you hike this trail, plan to spend some time at the lake, soaking in its beauty if not its frigid waters. When ready to return, just retrace your steps to the trailhead.

13
STEVENS CREEK

Type of hike: Out-and-back.
Total distance: 1.4 miles (2.2 kilometers)
Best months: Late May–October.
Maps: USGS Mount Rainier East; Trails Illustrated: Mount Rainier National Park; Astronaut's Vista: Mount Rainier National Park; Washington, Earthwalk Press Hiking Map & Guide.
Starting point: Box Canyon Picnic Area.

General description: A one-hour hike in the southern section of the park which leads to two different unnamed falls along the same river.

Finding the trailhead: From the Stevens Canyon Entrance Station, drive 10.8 miles west on Stevens Canyon Road to the Box Canyon Picnic Area on the left (0.3 mile past the Box Canyon wayside exhibit). The hike begins here.

Parking & trailhead facilities: The Box Canyon Picnic Area has a large parking lot, restrooms, and picnic tables. For running water, go to the Box Canyon wayside exhibit, 0.3 mile east on Stevens Canyon Road.

Stevens Creek

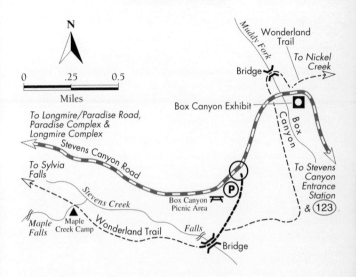

Key points:
0.5   (0.8)   River View Point.
0.6   (1.0)   Wonderland Trail junction.
0.7   (1.1)   Stevens Creek crossing.

The hike: This trail descends rather steeply through woods that abound with wildlife to two unnamed falls. The trail is well marked and well maintained, and you should reach the falls with no difficulty or confusion. The first point of interest comes after only 0.5 mile of downhill hiking. A sign marks the river view point to your right (west). Only a few paces more, and you stand in a fenced clearing, admiring the falls.

Return to the main trail and head right (south) to see the other nameless falls. Walk 0.1 mile beyond the river Viewpoint, a total of 0.6 mile from the trailhead, to a junction with the famed Wonderland Trail. Stay to the right (southwest) for another 0.1 mile to reach the bridge over Stevens Creek.

This bridge marks an incredible meeting of stream and stone. Iceberg white water rushing from the glaciers above has rounded these boulders and shaped them into something out of a fairy tale.

When you have appreciated the falls to your content, turn around and follow the same path back to the picnic area. The returning trail is not long, but it is a rather steep ascent, so do not be surprised if you are winded by the end.

14
BOX CANYON

Type of hike: Loop.
Total distance: 0.3 mile (0.5 kilometer).
Best months: May–September
Maps: USGS Mount Rainier East; Trails Illustrated: Mount Rainier National Park; Astronaut's Vista: Mount Rainier National Park; Washington, Earthwalk Press Hiking Map & Guide.
Starting point: Box Canyon.

General description: A very short loop that takes you over a canyon carved by a powerful glacier.

Finding the trailhead: From the Stevens Entrance Station, drive 10.5 miles west on Stevens Canyon Road to the Box Canyon Wayside Exhibit. Park on the left (south). If you pass the Box Canyon Picnic Area, which is 0.3 mile from the exhibit, you have gone too far. The paved trail is across the street from the parking lot to the right (east) of the bridge.

Parking & trailhead facilities: The Box Canyon Wayside Exhibit has a large parking lot, restrooms, and picnic tables. Water is available at the Box Canyon Wayside Exhibit, 0.3 mile east on Stevens Canyon Road.

Box Canyon

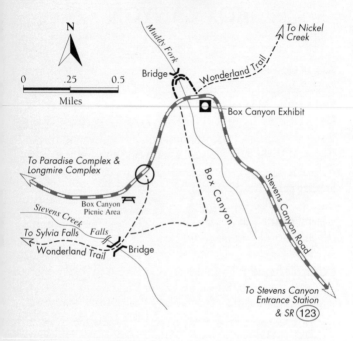

The hike: This hike is great for those interested in glaciers. A glacier gouged dirt and boulders out of the mountainside to create Box Canyon many years ago. The paved trail takes you past wildflowers, when in bloom, and past the thundering canyon itself. For the first half of this hike, the paved trail is wide, smooth, and wheelchair-accessible. The whole hike is in fact paved, eliminating most mud and muck, although the second half of the loop is considerably rougher.

At the trailhead, there is an informational sign about the hike. After reading it, head straight up the trail. Look for a trail merging from the right (northeast). This is the Wonderland Trail. Notice the bare rocks on the right side of the canyon where a powerful glacier wiped out most of the vegetation.

Less than 0.2 mile from the trailhead, a bridge crosses Muddy Fork. Take the time to look down and enjoy the unique canyon. After you cross the bridge, the trail is paved but less maintained all the way to the road. You can retrace your steps to the trailhead or walk along the road to loop back to your car.

15
SILVER FALLS

Type of hike: Loop.
Total distance: 2.7 miles (4.3 kilometers).
Best months: May–September.
Maps: USGS Ohanapecosh Hot Springs; Trails Illustrated: Mount Rainier National Park; Astronaut's Vista: Mount Rainier National Park; Washington, Earthwalk Press Hiking Map & Guide.
Starting point: Silver Falls Loop Trailhead.

General description: A short hike through beautiful forest to spectacular Silver Falls.

Finding the trailhead: From Stevens Canyon Entrance Station, drive 1.8 miles south on Washington Highway 123 to the turnoff for Ohanapecosh Campground. Turn right (west) and immediately right again where the road forks. Continue north toward the campground and past the visitor center until you come to another junction. Again, go right (north) toward the day parking lot, immediately to the right. You must loop around to the lot entrance on the east side. As you loop around, watch for Silver Falls Loop Trailhead on the left (north). Park and walk back to the trailhead.

Silver Falls

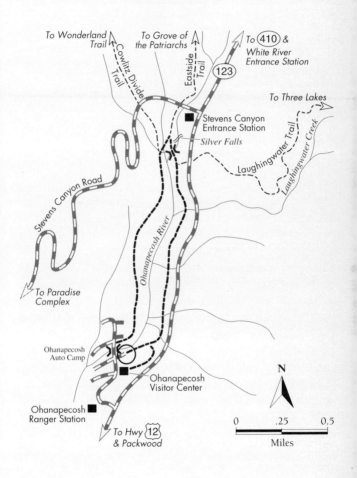

To Wonderland Trail

Cowlitz Divide Trail

To Grove of the Patriarchs

Eastside Trail

To (410) &
White River
Entrance Station

123

To Three Lakes

Stevens Canyon
Entrance Station

Silver Falls

Laughingwater Trail

Laughingwater Creek

Stevens Canyon Road

Ohanapecosh River

To Paradise
Complex

Ohanapecosh
Auto Camp

Ohanapecosh
Visitor Center

Ohanapecosh
Ranger Station

To Hwy (12)
& Packwood

N

0   .25   0.5
Miles

Parking & trailhead facilities: Restrooms are located at the Ohanapecosh Visitor Center. Remember to park in day parking to avoid all fines.

Key points:
0.1 (0.2) Junction with Hot Springs Trail.
1.0 (1.6) Junction with Laughingwater Trail.
1.2 (1.9) Silver Falls.
1.4 (2.2) Eastside Trail junction.
1.5 (2.4) Cowlitz Divide Trail junction.
2.7 (4.3) Ohanapecosh Campground.

The hike: Silver Falls opens early in the year due to its low elevation, so visitors can enjoy the falls as early as May. The trail wanders through a beautiful forest. The traffic can be very heavy on this trail, because the trailhead is located at Ohanapecosh Campground.

The first 0.1 mile of this hike is also part of an educational self-guided trail. The numbered posts correspond to an interpretive pamphlet that explains the Mount Rainier ecosystem. This is available at the Ohanapecosh Visitor Center. Stay left (north) when the Hot Springs Trail forks off to the right.

The beginning of the trail runs through a thermal area. You will see hot springs and interpretive signs about the thermal features. The ground is fragile and easily damaged here, making it especially important that you stay on the trail. Walking off the trail in this area is illegal and violators may be cited. Water originating from hot springs is unsafe for human consumption.

The trail gains a bit of elevation in the beginning and crosses two bridges before reaching the bridge over Laughingwater Creek. The first bridge is over 0.2 mile into your hike and the second bridge is a little less than 0.8 mile into your hike. Both of these bridges cross streams that empty into the Ohanapecosh River, which is to your left (west). At 0.9 mile, you reach Laughingwater Creek. It is easy to see where the creek gets its name as the water bounces and frolics over the rocks. After crossing Laughingwater Creek, you come to the Laughingwater Trail junction in 0.1 mile. Stay to the left and on the Silver Falls Loop.

It is only another 0.2 mile to the falls from the Laughingwater Trail junction, a total of 1.2 miles into your hike. An overlook, 0.1 mile from where you first see the falls, affords a view of Silver Falls' shining waters. Take your time and enjoy the marvelous view until you are ready to move on. The rocks at Silver Falls are moss-covered and slippery. People have died as a result of slipping on the rocks and falling. Please stay behind the guard rails.

The second half of the loop is not as eventful as the first half, but the trail winds through a pleasant mixture of western hemlock, Douglas-fir, and western redcedar. The trail exits in a different location from where it began, but simply walk over the bridge and head back to the day parking lot.

16
GROVE OF THE PATRIARCHS

Type of hike: Loop.
Total distance: 1.1 miles (1.8 kilometers).
Best months: May–September.
Maps: USGS Ohanapecosh Hot Springs; Trails Illustrated: Mount Rainier National Park; Astronaut's Vista: Mount Rainier National Park; Washington, Earthwalk Press Hiking Map & Guide.
Starting point: Eastside Trailhead.

General description: A short interpretive hike through magnificent old-growth forest.

Finding the trailhead: From Stevens Canyon Entrance Station, go 0.2 mile west on Stevens Canyon Road and pull into the parking lot on the right (north). The trailhead is to the left (west) of the restrooms.

Parking & trailhead facilities: Grove of the Patriarchs has a fairly big parking lot, but it is almost always packed. There are wheelchair-accessible restrooms located at the trailhead.

The hike: The trail is very well maintained, but often muddy. Wear your hiking boots and remember to step through the mud instead of around it to avoid widening the trails. Educational signs line the trail, helping you identify the difference

Grove of the Patriarchs

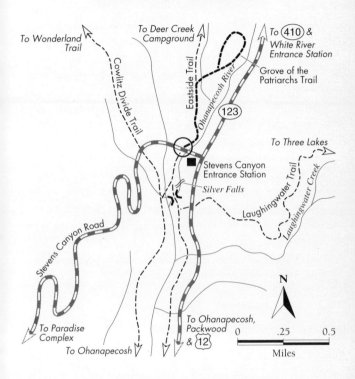

To Wonderland Trail

To Deer Creek Campground

To (410) & White River Entrance Station

Grove of the Patriarchs Trail

Cowlitz Divide Trail

Eastside Trail

Ohanapecosh River

(123)

To Three Lakes

Stevens Canyon Entrance Station

Silver Falls

Laughingwater Trail

Laughingwater Creek

Stevens Canyon Road

N

To Paradise Complex

To Ohanapecosh

To Ohanapecosh, Packwood & U.S. 12

0 .25 0.5

Miles

between western hemlock, Douglas-fir, and western red cedar. This is a great trail to take to learn more about the complexities of old-growth forests.

The trail begins to the right of the restrooms, heading north. For the first 0.3 mile, the Ohanapecosh River runs along the right side of the trail through old-growth forest.

It is abnormally clear for a glacial river because the Ohanapecosh glaciers are relatively inactive, reducing the amount of glacial flour suspended in the river. If it is a sunny day, you can see the sun sparkling off its clear surface.

The trail forks 0.3 mile into the hike. The trail continues heading north and the Grove of the Patriarchs trail veers off to the right (southeast) toward a steel suspension bridge over the Ohanapecosh River. The bridge leads to an island rich with old-growth forest. Some of the trees are more than 1,000 years old, towering over the forest floor.

Around 0.1 mile past the Grove of the Patriarchs junction, the trail splits to form a loop. Go left (northeast) around the loop. Make sure to check out the big cedar tree just over halfway through the loop. The enormity of the cedar tree is very humbling. Then continue along the loop until it rejoins itself. Retrace your steps from here to the trailhead. The return trip will give you a chance to apply the knowledge of trees you have just gained.

17
NACHES PEAK

Type of hike: Loop.
Total distance: 5.0 miles (8.3 kilometers).
Best months: Late July–September.
Maps: USGS Chinook Pass; Trails Illustrated: Mount Rainier National Park; Astronaut's Vista: Mount Rainier National Park; Washington, Earthwalk Press Hiking Map & Guide.
Starting point: Naches Peak Trailhead.

General description: A popular loop in the late summer, the Naches Peak Trail offers small mountain lakes, subalpine forest, good views of Mount Rainier, and a worthwhile side trip to Dewey Lake.

Finding the trailhead: Walk from Chinook Pass on Washington Highway 410 just outside the western boundary of the park. Park in the Tipsoo Lake parking lot, just west of Chinook Pass. Walk west along the highway for less than 0.5 mile to the large park entrance sign above the road. The top of the sign doubles as a hiking bridge, and the signed Naches Peak Trailhead is on the north side of the bridge.

Parking & trailhead facilities: The parking lot has a few toilets. The Tipsoo Picnic Area at the end of the loop has tables.

Naches Peak

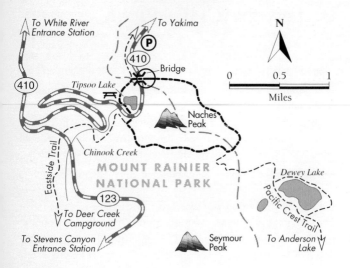

Key points:
2.2 (3.5) Pacific Crest Trail and Tipsoo Lake Trail junction.
4.6 (7.4) WA 410.
4.7 (7.5) Tipsoo Lake.
5.0 (8.0) WA 410.

The hike: For good reason, the loop around Naches Peak is a very popular hike. The first 2 miles of trail are outside park boundaries and along the Pacific Crest Trail. Because this trail is pet-friendly, you can see many hikers accompanied by leashed dogs of all varieties and the occasional horseback rider. If you have a pet you would like to walk, however, you cannot complete the loop. Pets are not allowed on the parts of the trail inside of the park, so hikers with pets should turn around before the entrance signs, where the Naches Peak Trail intersects with the Pacific Crest Trail.

From the Naches Peak Trailhead, cross the bridge to the other side (southeast) of WA 410. The trail ascends steadily and passes a few small subalpine lakes. Trails lead to the lakes, but they are not maintained and trekking through such fragile meadow is discouraged. Stay on the trail.

The highest point on the trail comes just before you enter the park. At this point, the trail curves eastward. Soon, 2.2 miles into the hike, the trail intersects with the trail returning to the area. To go to Tipsoo Lake or return to your car, stay to the right (east) here. Just as you round the bend, you catch a great view of Mount Rainier. To complete the Naches Peak loop, stay on the Pacific Crest Trail going left (south).

The trail wraps around Naches Peak to the right. Wildflowers blanket the meadows in midsummer and huckleberries do the same in late summer. You also pass a small mountain lake (not Tipsoo) on this side of the peak. When the trail turns north, you can see Tipsoo Lake with parking lot and picnic tables.

Before you can reach the picnic area, 4.7 miles into the hike, you must cross WA 410. The continuing trail is visible across the road. A different maintained trail loops around Tipsoo Lake, if care for a casual stroll.

The steepest incline on the hike is left for the end. The trail passes just north of the picnic area, switches back a few times, then sets you back at the trailhead. Walk east along WA 410 to return to your car.

18
DEGE PEAK

Type of hike: Out-and-back.
Total distance: 2.8 miles (4.5 kilometers).
Best months: Mid-July - September
Maps: USGS White River; Trails Illustrated: Mount Rainier National Park; Astronaut's Vista: Mount Rainier National Park; Washington, Earthwalk Press Hiking Map & Guide.
Starting point: Sunrise Point.
General description: A short climb to the top of Dege Peak with views of Mount Rainier, the North Cascades, Mount Adams, Mount Baker, and Sunrise Lake.

Finding the trailhead: From the White River Entrance Station, drive 11.3 miles up White River Road to the Sunrise Point Turnout.

Parking & trailhead facilities: There is a sizable parking lot at Sunrise Point, but it is always busy. A small chance exists that you might not find a parking spot. If the parking lot is full, parking along the road is not an option. Instead, consider the trail that climbs Dege Peak from the west side. (See Options.)

Key points:
1.1 (1.8) Junction with the spur trail to Dege Peak.
1.4 (2.2) Dege Peak summit.

Dege Peak

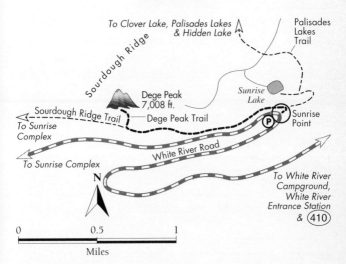

The hike: Although this hike is only 2.8 miles long, it is all uphill for the first 1.4 miles to Dege Peak. Make sure to bring plenty of water and pace yourself throughout the climb. From the top of Dege Peak, jaw-dropping scenery surrounds you in every direction.

The Sourdough Ridge Trail is located at the northwest end of the Sunrise Point parking lot across the White River Road. Head west on the Sourdough Ridge Trail. Wildflowers, such as lupine and magenta paintbrush, often line the trail in midsummer, and trees provide much-needed shade on a hot day. Look for Marcus Peak to the right (north) and, when you have gained enough elevation, Mount Rainier to the west.

After hiking 1.1 miles, you come to the junction with the Dege Peak Trail. Turn right (northeast) on this trail. It is only 0.3 mile to the summit from this point, but the trail follows steep switchbacks all the way to the top. At the top of Dege Peak, you have entered the alpine zone. The peak consists of rock; little vegetation grows on the rocky surface. You can see two dormant volcanoes, Mount Baker and Mount Adams, and enjoy an impressive view of majestic Mount Rainier.

When you decide to head back, it is all downhill! Relish the view of Clover and Sunrise Lakes as you descend the peak. Sunrise Lake is the closest of the two to Sunrise Point, where you began your hike, and Clover Lake is farther north, near Marcus Peak.

Options: If the parking lot is full or you want to start from the Sunrise area, park in the Sunrise parking lot, 2.6 miles from Sunrise Point on White River Road. There is a huge parking lot there, but on a sunny weekend it might be full. In this case, you might have to choose an alternate hike.

Head up the paved path to the right of the restrooms, leading to the Sourdough Ridge Nature Trail. Turn right (northeast) up the trail and stay on it for a little over 0.3 mile to the junction with Sourdough Ridge Trail. Turn right (east) onto the Sourdough Ridge Trail and head east toward Dege Peak, which is 1.5 miles away. This option has a total distance of 3.8 miles (6.1 kilometers).

19
SOURDOUGH RIDGE NATURE TRAIL

Type of hike: Loop.
Total distance: 1.5 miles (2.4 kilometers).
Best months: Mid-July–September.
Maps: USGS Sunrise; Trails Illustrated: Mount Rainier National Park; Astronaut's Vista: Mount Rainier National Park; Washington, Earthwalk Press Hiking Map & Guide.
Starting point: Sunrise complex.

General description: A one-hour self-guiding informative stroll along Sourdough Ridge.

Finding the trailhead: From the White River Entrance Station, drive 13.8 miles west on the White River Road and park at the Sunrise parking lot. The trailhead is to the north, to the right of the restrooms.

Parking &trailhead facilities: Even though the Sunrise complex offers a large parking lot, it fills beyond capacity on some sunny weekends. Visitors are turned away. Some circle the lot hoping for a vacant spot. The Sunrise complex has a variety of facilities, including running water, a cafeteria, restrooms, a gift shop, and a museum.

Sourdough Ridge Nature Trail

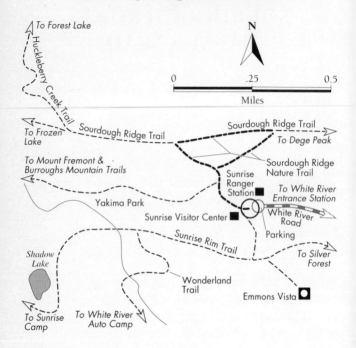

The hike: To begin this hike, go to the northwestern part of the parking lot. Follow the wide trail that runs north beyond the restrooms. About 0.1 mile into the hike, stop to look at the map and display on the right (east). The map delineates some of the trails in the Sunrise area, and includes elevation charts and short descriptions. Left of this map stands a small post with pamphlets for the Sourdough

Ridge Nature Trail, entitled "Sourdough Ridge: Subalpine Meadow Ecology." If you plan to keep this pamphlet, put 50 cents in the fee box. Otherwise, return the pamphlet upon completion of the hike.

Continue north on this trail until it forks. A sign points to the right (east); follow it. For information stations 1 through 7, you walk along the south slope of Sourdough Ridge. You have a fantastic view of the grandeur of Mount Rainier, while the stations inform you about the small but crucial parts of the ecosystem.

After station 7 the path forks; turn left (west). From stations 8 to 13, you walk along the top of Sourdough Ridge. You have a view of both sides of the ridge. On a clear day, you can see Mount Baker, Mount Adams, and Glacier Peak.

After post 13, turn left (south). The Sunrise complex comes into sight as the loop reaches its end. As the pamphlet says, "We hope this walk has given you a look behind the scenery, into the ever changing environmental forces that influence this subalpine community."

20
SILVER FOREST

Type of hike: Out-and-back.
Total distance: 2.0 miles (3.2 kilometers).
Best months: Mid-July–September.
Maps: USGS Sunrise and White River Basin; Trails Illustrated: Mount Rainier National Park; Astronaut's Vista: Mount Rainier National Park; Washington, Earthwalk Press Hiking Map & Guide.
Starting point: Sunrise complex.

General description: An easy one-hour walk to informative viewpoints and a flowery subalpine meadow.

Finding the trailhead: From the White River Entrance Station, drive 13.8 miles west on the White River Road to the Sunrise parking lot. Park in one of the many spaces provided. The trailhead is south of the parking lot.

Parking & trailhead facilities: Even though the Sunrise complex offers a large parking lot, it fills beyond capacity on some sunny weekends. Visitors are turned away. Some circle the lot hoping for a vacancy. The Sunrise complex also has a variety of facilities, including running water, a cafeteria, restrooms, a gift shop, and a museum.

Silver Forest

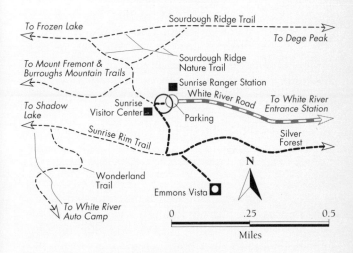

Key points:

0.1 (0.2) Sunrise Rim Trail junction.
0.2 (0.3) Emmons Vista Exhibits.
1.0 (1.6) End of maintained trail.

The hike: The Silver Forest Trail involves two parts. First, a short descent leads to two informative exhibits with great views of Mount Rainier. Then, the trail continues east through subalpine forest and meadow.

To find the trailhead, park in the Sunrise parking lot. At the south side of the lot, directly across from the ranger station and cafeteria, a trail heads south and a dirt road heads west. As the sign directs, follow the southbound trail, the Emmons Vista Nature Trail.

In only 0.1 mile you reach the junction with the Sunrise Rim Trail. Stay to the left (south). The path curves east and a sign points south to the first Emmons Vista exhibit. Walk down to the viewpoint and admire the tree-framed view of the Emmons and Winthrop Glaciers. The exhibit explains the various parts of a glaciated mountain and how they were formed.

Return to the main trail and continue east. You soon come upon the second exhibit, again immediately south of the trail. This vista point has a nice sheltered seating area and two more informative signs. The first, "Snow Shadow," includes climatic information about the winds and snow of Paradise. The other, "Rocks Riding on Air," gives a historical account of the Little Tahoma Peak rock-slide of 1963.

Back on the main trail, head east once again. In less than 0.1 mile you come to a sign indicating that you have reached the Silver Forest portion of the trail. A fire of unknown origins incinerated this area long ago. Now only the "silver sentinels," burned remnants, remain from the forest before the fire. In the fire's wake, subalpine trees and wildflowers have grown, making this forest particularly intriguing. Small gnarled trees are dispersed in this meadow along with blankets of violet flowers in midsummer. Walk along this trail for 0.8 mile before reaching a sign that indicates the end of the maintained trail, 1 mile into the hike. The trail continues for quite some distance beyond this sign, so venture farther if you want an extended hike. Otherwise, turn around and walk back to the Sunrise complex.

21
EMMONS MORAINE

Type of hike: Out-and-back.
Total distance: 2.8 miles (4.5 kilometers).
Best months: Early July–September.
Maps: USGS Sunrise and White River; Trails Illustrated: Mount Rainier National Park; Astronaut's Vista: Mount Rainier National Park; Washington, Earthwalk Press Hiking Map & Guide.
Starting point: Glacier Basin Trailhead.

General description: A short hike up to the Emmons Moraine with an excellent view of the Emmons Glacier, the largest glacier in the contiguous United States.

Finding the trailhead: From the White River Entrance Station, drive 3.9 miles to the White River Campground turnoff. Turn left (northwest) toward the campground and drive 1.2 miles to the parking area on the left. A sign indicates that the parking lot is for backpackers and climbers. Park here and walk to loop D. This is one of the many loops that make up White River Campground. In the middle of loop D, you will find the Glacier Basin Trailhead.

Parking & trailhead facilities: There are restrooms along loop C and a pay phone at the entrance.

Emmons Moraine

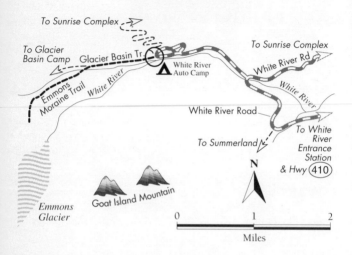

The hike: This short, gradual uphill hike is great for children. You hike along the Emmons Moraine for a close-up view of Emmons Glacier. At one time, the Emmons Glacier filled the whole valley here. The glacier carved an amazingly flat and expansive section out of the earth.

From the Glacier Basin Trailhead, head west along the Glacier Basin Trail. Very near the beginning of the trail, you come to an informational billboard about this hike and other hikes in the immediate area. From here, hike 0.9 mile through tranquil forest to the junction with Emmons Moraine Trail. At the junction, go left (southwest) up the Emmons Moraine Trail.

Continue slightly uphill for another 0.5 mile to the end of the maintained trail. Your feet sink into the sandy trail formed from silt deposits by the Emmons Glacier. On a hot day, the sand soaks up the sun, adding to the scorching heat. Also, the little trees along Emmons Moraine provide little or no shade. Be sure to bring sunscreen. When you have marveled at the Emmons Glacier long enough, head back the same way you came.

22
MOUNT FREMONT LOOKOUT

Type of hike: Out-and-back.
Total distance: 5.4 miles (8.6 kilometers).
Best months: Late July–September.
Maps: USGS Sunrise and White River; Trails Illustrated: Mount Rainier National Park; Astronaut's Vista: Mount Rainier National Park; Washington, Earthwalk Press Hiking Map & Guide.
Starting point: Sunrise complex.

General description: A short ascent to a fire lookout on Mount Fremont that towers over the north side of the park and has great views of Mount Rainier, Skyscrape Mountain, Grand Park, and Sourdough Ridge.

Finding the trailhead: From the White River Entrance Station, drive 13.8 miles west on White River Road to the Sunrise parking lot. Park and walk to the trailhead to the right of the restrooms.

Parking & trailhead facilities: You should not have trouble finding a parking spot unless it is a sunny weekend, in which case you might have to choose an alternate hike. A number of facilities are located at the Sunrise complex, such as restrooms, a pay phone, a restaurant, and a gift shop.

Mount Fremont Lookout

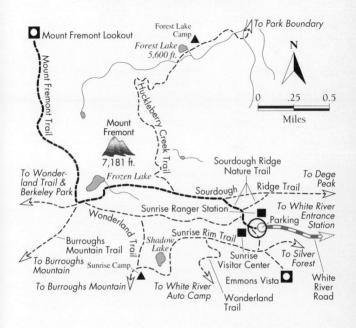

Key points:

0.1	(0.2)	Sourdough Ridge Nature Trail junction.
0.3	(0.5)	Sourdough Ridge Trail junction.
0.6	(1.0)	Huckleberry Creek Trail junction.
1.4	(2.2)	Mount Fremont Trail junction.
2.7	(4.3)	Mount Fremont Lookout.

The hike: Walk up the paved path to the right (east) of the restrooms until the trail forks. Take the dirt trail on the right heading north. Get on that trail and travel north until you come to the junction with Sourdough Nature Trail. Turn left (northwest) onto the Sourdough Ridge Nature Trail and walk 0.2 mile to the Sourdough Ridge Trail. Turn left (west) onto the Sourdough Ridge Trail.

While you are walking along the Sourdough Ridge Trail, you can see the North Cascades to your right. Mount Rainier also looks magnificent from Sourdough Ridge. After 0.3 mile you pass the Huckleberry Creek Trail on your right, heading northwest. Keep going for another 0.8 mile to a five-way junction, immediately after Frozen Lake. The Mount Fremont Trail is the first trail on the right. Head north on it. At this point, you will travel above timberline for the rest of the hike. Fat marmots inhabit the green meadows along the trail. Keep in mind that it is illegal to feed animals and detrimental to their survival skills.

Soon you will be walking along the rocky side of Mount Fremont. Watch your step—the ledge drops straight off the ridge! Low-growing subalpine wildflowers line the trail in late July. Walk along the ridge until you reach the lookout, 2.7 miles from the Sunrise complex. From the lookout, you can see all the way to the north end of the park, where the clearcuts start. Skyscrape Mountain is to your left and Mount Rainier towers above it all. Take the time to get out your map, look around, and identify the landmarks around you.

23
FOREST LAKE

Type of hike: Out-and-back.
Total distance: 5.0 miles (8.0 kilometers).
Best months: Late July–September.
Maps: USGS Sunrise and White River; Trails Illustrated Mount Rainier National Park; Astronaut's Vista: Mount Rainier National Park; Washington, Earthwalk Press Hiking Map & Guide.
Starting Point: Sunrise parking lot.

General description: A short descent that passes over a rocky alpine terrain, through subalpine meadows, to a quaint mountain lake.

Finding the trailhead: From the White River Entrance Station, drive 13.8 miles west on the White River Road to the Sunrise Parking lot. Park there and walk to the trailhead, to the right of the restrooms.

Parking & trailhead facilities: You should have no trouble finding a parking spot unless it is a sunny weekend, in which case you might have to choose an alternate hike. A number of facilities are located at the Sunrise complex, such as restrooms, a pay phone, a restaurant, and a gift shop.

Forest Lake

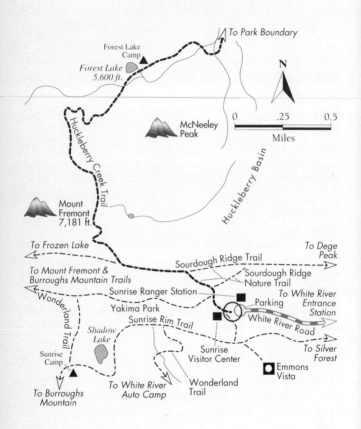

To Park Boundary

Forest Lake Camp

Forest Lake
5,600 ft.

N

McNeeley Peak

0   .25   0.5
Miles

Huckleberry Creek Trail

Huckleberry Basin

Mount Fremont
7,181 ft.

To Frozen Lake

Sourdough Ridge Trail

To Dege Peak

To Mount Fremont &
Burroughs Mountain Trails

Sourdough Ridge
Nature Trail

Wonderland Trail

Sunrise Ranger Station

To White River
Entrance
Station

Parking

Yakima Park

White River Road

Shadow Lake

Sunrise Rim Trail

Sunrise Camp

Sunrise
Visitor Center

To Silver Forest

To Burroughs
Mountain

To White River
Auto Camp

Wonderland
Trail

Emmons
Vista

Key points:
0.1   (0.2)   Sourdough Nature Trail junction.
0.3   (0.5)   Sourdough Ridge Trail junction.
0.6   (1.0)   Huckleberry Creek Trail junction.
2.5   (4.0)   Forest Lake and Forest Lake Camp.

The hike: If you want to escape the crowd at Sunrise and experience a variety of different ecosystems, this is the hike for you. From the tundra on the north side of Sourdough Ridge to the deciduous forest that surrounds Forest Lake, you will have a taste of everything.

Walk up the paved path to the right (east) of the restrooms until the trail forks. Take the dirt trail on your right (north). Get on that trail and walk up it until you come to the junction with Sourdough Nature Trail. Turn left (northwest) onto the Sourdough Nature Trail and walk 0.2 mile to the Sourdough Ridge Trail. Turn left (west) onto the Sourdough Ridge Trail.

While you are walking along the Sourdough Ridge Trail, you can see the Cascades to the north. Mount Rainier also looks magnificent from Sourdough Ridge. Soon you will come to the Huckleberry Creek Trail on your right. Follow the Huckleberry Creek Trail as it climbs briefly and then begins its long descent to Forest Lake. The first part of the trail is in the alpine zone and relatively rocky. There are low-growing wildflowers, such as red mountain heather, all around. Be aware that patches of snow might stay on the trail until August, but the trail is usually easy to follow.

We saw a lot of mountain goat tracks on this trail, so keep your eyes open for mountain goats on both Mount

Fremont, to your left, and McNeeley Peak, to your right. The lush Huckleberry Basin is south of McNeeley Peak, visible from Sourdough Ridge.

Soon the trail heads into the trees and wanders through forest and meadows, overflowing with wildflowers in late July, all the way to Forest Lake. Forest Lake is small, but charming. There is a great place right next to the campsite to take a break and enjoy the lake. Retrace your tracks to return to the trailhead.

24
SUNRISE RIM

Type of hike: Loop.
Total distance: 4.9 miles (7.8 kilometers).
Best months: August– September.
Maps: USGS Sunrise and White River; Trails Illustrated: Mount Rainier National Park; Astronaut's Vista: Mount Rainier National Park; Washington, Earthwalk Press Hiking Map & Guide.
Starting point: Sunrise complex.

General description: A loop that takes you by Shadow Lake, over the first hump of Burroughs Mountain, and to an overlook of Emmons Glacier.

Finding the trailhead: From the White River Entrance Station, drive 13.8 miles west on the White River Road to the Sunrise parking lot. Park and walk to the trailhead north of the road and to the right of the restrooms.

Parking & trailhead facilities: You should not have trouble finding a parking spot unless it is a sunny weekend, in which case you might have to choose an alternate hike. A number of facilities are located at the Sunrise complex, such as restrooms, a pay phone, a restaurant, and a gift shop.

Sunrise Rim

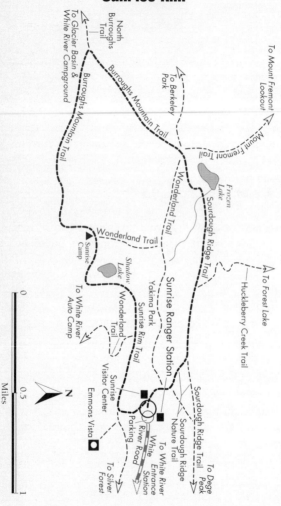

North
Burroughs
Trail

To Glacier Basin &
White River Campground

Burroughs Mountain Trail

Burroughs Mountain Trail

To Berkeley
Park

To Mount Fremont
Lookout

Mount Fremont Trail

Frozen
Lake

Wonderland Trail

Sourdough Ridge Trail

Sunrise
Camp

Shadow
Lake

To White River
Auto Camp

Wonderland Trail

Sunrise Rim Trail

Yakima Park

Sunrise Ranger Station

To Forest Lake

Huckleberry Creek Trail

To Dege
Peak

Sourdough Ridge Trail

Sourdough Ridge Nature Trail

Sunrise
Visitor Center

To White River
Entrance Station

White River Road

Parking

To Silver
Forest

Emmons Vista

0

0.5

1

Miles

N

90

Key points:

0.1 (0.2) Junction with Sourdough Nature Trail.
0.3 (0.5) Junction with Sourdough Ridge Trail.
0.6 (1.0) Junction with Huckleberry Creek Trail.
1.4 (2.2) Junction with Burroughs Mountain Trail.
2.1 (3.4) First hump of Burroughs Mountain.
3.4 (5.4) Sunrise Camp/junction with Sunrise Rim Trail.
3.6 (5.8) Shadow Lake.
4.4 (7.0) Junction with Wonderland Trail.
4.9 (7.8) Sunrise parking lot.

The hike: Great for kids and adults alike, this hike explores the scenic area around the Sunrise complex. You walk along Sourdough Ridge, climb to the first hump of Burroughs Mountain, and look over Emmons Glacier. It is rare to cover such a wide range of landscapes and see such incredible views in such a short hike.

Walk up the paved path to the right (east) of the restrooms until you see a fork in the trail. Take the dirt trail on your right heading north. Get on the trail and walk up it until you come to the junction with the Sourdough Ridge Nature Trail. Turn left (northwest) onto the Sourdough Ridge Nature Trail and walk 0.2 mile to the Sourdough Ridge Trail. Then, turn left (west) onto the Sourdough Ridge Trail.

While you are walking along this trail, you can see the Cascades to your right and on really clear days you can even see Mount Baker. Mount Rainier also looks magnificent from Sourdough Ridge. You will walk a total of 0.3 mile along the ridge, 0.6 mile from the Sunrise complex, to the

Huckleberry Creek Trail on your right, heading northwest. Stay to the left and on the Sourdough Ridge Trail for another 0.8 mile to the junction with Burroughs Mountain Trail. Directly before the junction, you pass Frozen Lake to the right (north). As the signs tell you, Frozen Lake is a domestic water supply; the National Park Service has fenced in the lake to avoid possible contamination by humans. The fence is not very aesthetically pleasing, but a necessity.

Once you have reached the five-trail junction, take the Burroughs Mountain Trail, which heads southwest. Steep snowfields cover this trail into August some years. Sturdy boots and an ice ax are recommended. The trail up to the first hump of Burroughs Mountain gains about 200 feet and travels into alpine terrain. The vegetation in this area is very fragile and susceptible to human impact. Please stay on the trail to avoid damaging the delicate ecosystem.

From Burroughs Mountain, look northwest to see Old Desolate and north to Berkeley Park. Old Desolate is a barren plateau that sticks out among forested hills. It is quite a contrast to the bright wildflowers that fill Berkeley Park.

When you reach the first hump of Burroughs Mountain, 0.7 mile from Frozen Lake, turn left (east). To the south, you see Emmons Glacier, the largest glacier in the contiguous United States. A better view of the glacier comes from the glacier overlook, 1.1 miles away. It is all downhill to the overlook and all the way to Sunrise Camp.

You can see all of Emmons Glacier and the beginning of White River from the glacial overlook. Goat Island Mountain towers above both of these natural wonders. White River originates from Emmons Glacier and is filled with sediment and glacial flour deposited from the glacier. Notice that there are several pools in the valley below. These pools appear sea foam green due to the large concentration of sediment suspended in their waters. The sun reflects light off of the cloudy waters to produce this gorgeous color. It is amazing to imagine that the valley below you once contained the whole Emmons Glacier. Global warming has reduced the glacier to its present size, but all glaciers in the park are presently advancing.

From the glacial overlook, continue heading downhill to Sunrise Camp. To your left, an administrative road heads north and passes Sunrise Camp. You want to continue going east, but now on Sunrise Rim Trail instead of Burroughs Mountain Trail.

After hiking 0.2 mile east on the Sunrise Rim Trail and 3.6 miles into your hike, Shadow Lake appears to the left. Previous hikers have greatly damaged the area around Shadow Lake, the water source for Sunrise Camp. Again, please stay on the trail to reduce any further impact to the lake.

The remainder of the loop travels through the subalpine meadows of Yakima Park. In July and early August, Yakima Park is filled with a variety of wildflowers. At times, you can see Goat Island Mountain and the Emmons Glacier from the trail. The trail is flat until you intersect with the Wonderland Trail, and then it travels gradually uphill all the way to the Sunrise parking lot.

25
GREEN LAKE

Type of hike: Out-and-back.
Total distance: 3.6 miles (5.8 kilometers).
Best months: May–October.
Maps: USGS Carbon River; Trails Illustrated Mount Rainier National Park; Astronaut's Vista: Mount Rainier National Park; Washington, Earthwalk Press Hiking Map & Guide.
Starting point: Green Lake Trailhead.

General description: A moderate, two-hour hike past a waterfall to a small, pretty lake in the northwestern region of the park.

Finding the trailhead: From Carbon River Entrance Station, drive 3 miles east on Carbon River Road. The Green Lake Trailhead is between Ranger Creek to the right (south) and a small parking lot to the left (north).

Parking & trailhead facilities: The Green Lake Trailhead has few available spaces. Cars often line the road, parked on either side. There are no services here. For a pay phone and a restroom, go to the Carbon River Entrance Station, 3 miles west on Carbon River Road.

Green Lake

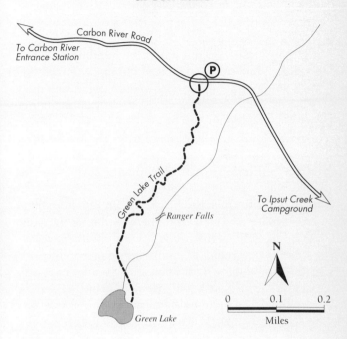

Key points:

1.0	(1.6)	Ranger Falls.
1.5	(2.4)	Ranger Creek Crossing.
1.8	(2.9)	Green Lake.

The hike: The hike to Green Lake attracts many late spring-hikers, because the snow clears earlier on this trail than most others in the park. Its traffic may lessen as the other trails open, but its charm does not.

Dense, green rain forest and the gurgling sound of streams surround you as you ascend this moderate hill. After only 1 mile, the gurgling turns to churning. A very short jaunt to the left (east) leads to a close-up view of Ranger Falls. Continue right to reach Green Lake.

Only 0.5 mile beyond Ranger Falls on the way to Green Lake, you must cross Ranger Creek. No fording is necessary, but the log bridge with only wire for a grip gets a bit slippery when wet, so cross carefully.

Less than 0.3 mile beyond the bridge, you come upon Green Lake. One glance, and the inspiration for the name becomes apparent. Surrounded by evergreens, the water reflects their emerald hue. The surrounding mountains shelter the water, keeping it placid on most days. From a small clearing at the trail's end, a nice view of Tolmie Peak can be seen across the lake. No trails run around the lake for further exploration, but the small clearing is a good place to picnic or just rest before descending along the same path.

Option: If you would rather not hike the full 3.6 miles round-trip, turning back at Ranger Falls shortens the hike to only 2 miles round-trip, and the falls still make the effort worthwhile.

26
TOLMIE PEAK

Type of hike: Out-and-back.
Total distance: 6.5 miles (10.4 kilometers).
Best months: Mid-July–September.
Maps: USGS Carbon River; Trails Illustrated: Mount Rainier National Park; Astronaut's Vista: Mount Rainier National Park; Washington, Earthwalk Press Hiking Map & Guide.
Starting point: Mowich Lake Campground.

General description: A very popular half-day hike through forest and meadow to a fire lookout atop Tolmie Peak with a spectacular view of the northwestern side of Mount Rainier.

Finding the trailhead: From the town of Wilkeson, drive south on Washington Highway 165. About 9 miles beyond Wilkeson, WA 165 intersects with the Carbon River Road. Stay to the right on WA 165. The pavement ends 3.2 miles beyond the intersection. Drive along the dirt road 8.8 miles to the park boundary, and continue 5.3 miles to Mowich Lake Campground, which has a small parking lot. Many trails originate here; the trail to Tolmie Peak (Wonderland Trail) is on the immediate left.

Tolmie Peak

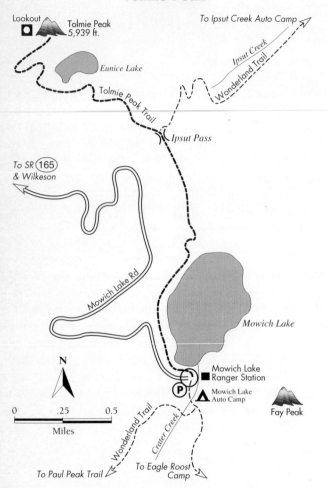

Lookout
Tolmie Peak
5,939 ft.

Eunice Lake

To Ipsut Creek Auto Camp

Ipsut Creek

Tolmie Peak Trail

Wonderland Trail

Ipsut Pass

*To SR (165)
& Wilkeson*

Mowich Lake Rd

Mowich Lake

N

0   .25   0.5
Miles

Mowich Lake
Ranger Station

P

Mowich Lake
Auto Camp

Fay Peak

Wonderland Trail

Crater Creek

To Paul Peak Trail

*To Eagle Roost
Camp*

Key points:

1.3 (2.2) Tolmie Peak Trail junction.
2.2 (3.5) Eunice Lake.
3.1 (5.0) Tolmie Peak Lookout.
3.2 (5.1) Tolmie Peak.

The hike: The hike to Tolmie Peak is one of the most popular in the park for many reasons. You do not have to pass through an entrance station to reach the trailhead, but be certain that you pay the required amount at the fee station, 12 miles after the intersection with Carbon River Road. The hike is not too long, nor too rigorous, and the rewards are immense. The view of Mount Rainier from Tolmie Peak is absolutely breathtaking.

From the Mowich Lake Campground, follow the trail to the left heading north. Walk along the trail hugging the west side of Mowich Lake about 0.5 mile before leaving the lakeside and heading northwest. After reaching the top of a small hill, continue 0.5 mile on flat terrain to the junction with the Tolmie Peak Trail. At the junction turn left (west).

The trail immediately begins to descend steeply. At the bottom of this hill, about 2 miles into the hike, the trail forks. The trail to the left is an unmaintained social trail created by those eager to see a rather unimpressive waterfall only a few paces off the beaten path. Stay to the right (north) to continue the journey to Eunice Lake and Tolmie Peak.

At this point, the trail begins a steep climb via switchbacks to Eunice Lake. In mid-July, as you approach Eunice Lake you step into a field blanketed by avalanche lilies. The lake's aqua waters are surrounded by jutting peaks and subalpine forest.

A sign points the way to Tolmie Peak and informs you that only 0.8 mile remains of the 3.1 miles total to the lookout. Stay to the left (west) on the marked trail around the lake. Those who have ventured off have spoiled the land, killing the fragile meadow plants and creating an array of ugly paths to the lake.

The trail reaches the northwestern part of the lake in 0.2 mile. It then begins to ascend by means of long switchbacks to the Tolmie Peak Lookout. The view from the lookout is spectacular. To the north, you see an expanse of rolling mountains. To the south, however, you see one of the best panoramic views of Mount Rainier available in the park.

The more adventurous can carefully walk the unmaintained trail along a ridge for 0.1 mile to the true Tolmie Peak. The trail is not steep, but it is rocky and a bit tricky at points.

Options: Rather than hiking all the way to the top of Tolmie Peak, you could go only as far as Eunice Lake. This option would cut 2 miles off the total distance. Eunice Lake is absolutely delightful, and the fields of avalanche lilies are amazing.

27
SPRAY FALLS

Type of hike: Out-and-back.
Total distance: 4.0 miles (6.4 kilometers).
Best months: Early July–September.
Maps: USGS Golden Lakes; Trails Illustrated: Mount Rainier National Park; Astronaut's Vista: Washington, Earthwalk Press Hiking Map & Guide.
Starting point: Mowich Lake parking lot.

General description: A short, relatively flat hike through the forest to the striking Spray Falls.

Finding the trailhead: From Wilkeson, drive 9 miles south on Washington Highway 165 to where the road forks. Stay to the right (south) at this fork, toward Mowich Lake. After 3.2 miles, the road turns into a well-maintained dirt road, although it can be very slippery when muddy. Follow this road another 8.8 miles to the Paul Peak Trailhead on the right (south) side of the road. There is a fee station located at the trailhead. Be sure to pay the entrance fee before heading up the road. Mowich Lake is another 5.3 miles up the gravel road, making it about 26.3 miles from Wilkeson.

Parking & trailhead facilities: There are restrooms at Mowich Lake. The parking lot is big, but on sunny weekends you might have to park along the road.

Spray Falls

To Tolmie Peak

To SR 165 & Wilkeson

To Ipsut Creek Auto Camp

Wonderland Trail

Mowich Lake Rd

Castle Peak

Mowich Lake

Mother Mountain

Mowich Lake Ranger Station

Mist Park

To Cataract Valley Camp

Wonderland Trail

Fay Peak

Mowich Lake Auto Camp

Mount Pleasant

Crater Creek

Hessong Rock

Grant Cr

Spray Park Trail

Spray Park

N

To Paul Peak Trail

Spray Creek

Eagle Roost Camp

Spray Falls

Spray Falls Trail

0   0.5   1

Miles

Key points:

0.2	(0.3)	Junction with the Spray Park Trail.
1.8	(2.9)	Junction with spur trail to Eagle Roost Camp.
1.9	(3.0)	Spray Falls Trail junction.
2.0	(3.2)	Spray Creek and view of Spray Falls.

The hike: This hike has no significant elevation gain, but rises and dips over rolling hills all the way to Spray Falls. The well-maintained, heavily used trail winds through beautiful forest. Expect to see many other park visitors. Please reduce your impact on the beautiful forest by staying on the trail.

Head to the south end of Mowich Lake, past the restrooms and the Mowich Lake Campground to the Wonderland Trail. Go south on the Wonderland Trail for a little over 0.2 mile to the junction with Spray Park Trail. Go left (southeast) when the Spray Park Trail forks off from the Wonderland Trail. There is a short spur trail 1.3 miles from the junction that takes you to an overlook from Eagle Cliff, a total of 1.5 miles into your hike. You can see the North Mowich Glacier clearly from the lookout.

When you have traveled 1.9 miles total, look for signs for Eagle Roost Camp. Eagle Roost Camp is less than 0.1 mile away and northwest of the Spray Park Trail. Just a bit beyond Eagle Roost Camp is the junction with Spray Falls Trail. Go right (southeast) on Spray Falls Trail and walk 0.1 mile to Spray Creek and the misty Spray Falls.

These awe-inspiring falls drop roughly 160 feet. At the top of the falls, the water sprays off the mossy rocks, leaving the air misty and cool. Lewis and yellow monkeyflowers line Spray Creek to add to the beauty of this natural wonder.

About the Authors

Heidi Schneider and Mary Skjelset make up the youngest author team to ever write a FalconGuide. Heidi has hiked extensively throughout the West with her family since high school and college and is currently attending Lewis and Clark College in Portland, Oregon. Mary also lives in Portland, where she studies political science at Reed College. When not writing or studying, she enjoys hiking (of course) and camping, skiing, dance, and soccer. They hiked all the trails of Mount Rainier National Park during the summer of 1998.